Camilla,

Hope these

of use in

sounded so nice on the

radio. Love from Charlie

xx

Five Steps to
Financial Wellbeing

Five Steps to Financial Wellbeing

How Changing Your Relationship with Money Can Change Your Whole Life

Clare Seal

For the financial misfits,
and for Phil, the ultimate teammate

First published in 2022 by HEADLINE HOME
An imprint of HEADLINE PUBLISHING GROUP

1

Cataloguing in Publication Data is available from the British Library

ISBN 978 1 4722 8920 9
eISBN 978 1 4722 8922 3

Designed and Typeset by Avon DataSet Ltd, Alcester, Warwickshire

Printed and bound in Great Britain by Clays Ltd, Elcograf S.p.A.

Headline's policy is to use papers that are natural, renewable and
recyclable products and made from wood grown in sustainable forests.
The logging and manufacturing processes are expected to conform to the
environmental regulations of the country of origin.

HEADLINE PUBLISHING GROUP
An Hachette UK Company
Carmelite House
50 Victoria Embankment
London EC4Y 0DZ

www.headline.co.uk
www.hachette.co.uk

Contents

Introduction

I would like to outlaw talking about wellbeing without addressing financial wellbeing.

It's always good to start a book with a bold statement, but it's true. Because it is very, *very* difficult to achieve a general state of wellbeing if that sense of peace and control doesn't extend to your financial life too. I'm not talking about being rich here. It's perfectly possible to live a happy and fulfilled life without abundant wealth (no matter what some people might tell you), and it's also possible to live a positively miserable life with millions in the bank. Money is not the be-all and end-all – in fact, there are lots of very essential things that it *can't* buy you – but it is very, *very* difficult to live a happy and fulfilled life if you are locked in a constant battle with your finances. Its effects ripple out into every corner of our lives, and it has the ability to put a strain on our relationships, affect our mental health and dictate the career and lifestyle choices that we make. So, this book is *not* about how to make more money. There are plenty of other volumes promising to make you rich, and you'll usually find them on bestseller lists. My promise is a more modest but, in my opinion, infinitely more valuable one. I want to help you to fix your relationship with money and, once you do that, I think a lot of other things will change for you. That's certainly what happened for me.

I started my own personal financial journey from a place of quite severe self-loathing. I had reached a complete breaking point, having neglected my relationship with money and financial wellbeing for over a decade. I was twenty-nine, a mother to two small children, and more than £27,000 in the red. Not only was my debt large, but it was spread across multiple accounts – credit cards, store cards and an overdraft – meaning that I had repayments pinging out of my accounts at all times of the month. Often, direct debits would be returned, complicating things even further, and it was only a matter of time before one or more of my spinning financial plates would crash to the ground. I was anxious, not sleeping well, preoccupied and irritable. I was aggressively ambitious at work, to the point where I was probably not a very good colleague, because I felt compelled to pursue financial success above everything else, so that I could fund a lifestyle that I believed would finally make me happy. I assumed that the world in which I was a successful, thin, beautiful and fulfilled person could be built out of material things, and material things cost money. At the same time, I was failing miserably in this pursuit, because both my priorities *and* my methods were off, which only served to further complicate and erode my relationship with money.

For the first ten years after I started managing my own money, I was very disconnected from my finances. I saw money only as a means to an end, and had a very distorted view of the value that things held. For some reason I really struggled to connect my actions with money to the way that I felt about it, and the anxiety and despondency that not having enough of it were causing me. I was stuck in cycles of behaviour that I knew were hurting me, damaging my chances at a secure future, and making me feel more and more ashamed and alone, but I didn't know how to break out of them. Every now and again I would try to apply my logical brain to my messy financial accounts, but real life would get in the way, and I didn't know how to reconcile the two. It took a rude awakening and brutal honesty, followed by a lot of reflection and work, to sort it out, but I got there in the end.

That is what I want you to get from this book. The tools, knowledge and support that you need to create some harmony between your brain and your bank balance, without having to conform to someone else's idea of what it means to be 'good with money'. To bridge that engagement gap between what you know and what you feel, and to help you to acknowledge, then challenge, the behaviours that are keeping you stuck in a toxic relationship with money.

There may be times during these five steps that you think we've veered off course a little, when you start to wonder what the topics and exercises we're discussing have to do with money. But you're going to have to trust me, because in order to make something work well, you have to exercise and strengthen the surrounding muscles too. Superficial fixes for financial problems are easy to come by – but all of the tips and tricks in the world won't fix a relationship with money that is fundamentally broken. The boundary between our finances and the rest of our lives, in so far as it exists, is porous in both directions; what we do with our money has an effect on everything else, but the way that we look after ourselves and the decisions that we make elsewhere affect our financial situation too.

Remember that your money doesn't exist in a vacuum

Money is also, of course, not just about personal finance. It is a political and societal issue, influencing – even deciding – the power structures in every sphere, from offices to governments. Our relationship with money as a species has a long history, and the societal narratives that have built up around wealth and hardship have been heavily influenced by everything from war to religion. We are encouraged to measure our success in pounds sterling, but it's important to remember that this path to 'success', as dictated by culture and society, isn't a running track. It's a treadmill, or a hamster wheel. There is no destination, so it's up to us to set our own paths, and to define our own ideas of success and happiness, financial and otherwise. This is actually fairly well-documented by psychologists, who call it the 'hedonic treadmill', a theory that explains, in part, why a sense of fulfilment and wellbeing is so difficult for people to achieve, especially when it comes to money. It's something that can be applied to several elements of our financial wellbeing, from spending to saving and to goal planning. We'll talk about this in greater detail a little later on.

I find that it's important to remember that money has a life of its own outside of your experience of it, because some things, such as generational wealth, nepotism, stagnating wages and exploding house prices, are just not within your control. There is a little comfort in that, because remembering the external influences on our financial wellbeing means that we don't accidentally take more responsibility for it than is healthy. Berating yourself for messing up something that you don't even have any control over is *not* a healthy way to live life, and that applies to money just as it applies to any other area. The good news is that acknowledging the factors that are not within our control means that we can better focus on those that are.

Despite its importance, our financial health is not something we're really taught to look after. It should be as elementary as basic hygiene, and yet we are often left to figure it out for ourselves, leaving many of us feeling confused and alone. To the bafflement of many people, including me, financial literacy is all but left out of the school curriculum in the UK, and where it *is* taught, it is often lacking in vital context or connection to other personal skills. For many, this results in a disconnect between money and the rest of our existence, which leaves us with a misunderstanding of the interplay between our wallets and our happiness. If there *is* a widely recognized connection between money and wellbeing, then it's simply whether we can afford a Peloton, say, or a far-flung holiday. This is, of course, part of it – but only a very small one. There is so much more to be explored and explained, from the impact of financial hardship on mental health to the damage that can be done by an unhealthy obsession with cash.

Even if you happen to be one of the lucky ones – someone whose parents have always taken an active interest in teaching you about money – there's no guarantee that you'll end up finding it easy, because the second that we are launched into the world of work and money, of earning and owning and owing, the whole playing field changes. We're faced with temptations and judgements, often simultaneously, that cloud our ability to make decisions and can quickly evaporate any confidence we might have had in our money-management skills, as well as any cash we might have. We are not warned early enough about how advertising will convince us that we're lacking something, in order to sell us yet another thing that we don't need. And it won't just happen once, but time and time again.

If this all sounds rather hopeless, then please don't worry – the aim of this book is to teach you how to navigate the internal factors while acknowledging the external ones, hopefully without making you feel judged, patronized or infantilized. Because this is the other issue with mainstream financial advice and information – it can be far too basic and numbers based, leaving us with a notebook full of sums and a mind full of worry.

Internal factors, external forces and the relationship between them

I thought for a long time about how to write a book that could inspire individual positive action without ignoring the fact that not everything is always under our personal control. For so many people, determination to take responsibility for every single thing that's gone wrong (or right) acts as a barrier to real change or even happiness. There is absolutely no point in accepting responsibility or blame for an issue that is simply not your fault, in the same way that it doesn't do you any favours to take credit for something that wasn't the result of your own efforts. If you have been paid very poorly, been the victim of a scam or financial abuse, been born into a family without wealth privilege or precedent, been discriminated against or experienced any number of other systemic injustices, that is not something for which you should be accepting responsibility. You can only change the things that are within your control, and that is what my five steps focus on, but you must always,

always acknowledge the ways in which external factors have played and continue to play a role in your relationship with money. Otherwise, you risk wasting valuable time and energy going round and round in circles, self-flagellating for things that aren't your fault. This is not about dwelling on your misfortunes or carrying a chip on your shoulder, just accepting and acknowledging those external forces at play in all of our lives and relieving yourself of any undue sense of responsibility for them.

Some of these external factors are systemic – they are built into the world in which we all have to operate, and they typically take a very long time to change. They affect us from childhood, providing a template for our relationship with money without us even really noticing until later on. There is still a huge gender pay gap, for example, which is greatly exaggerated for women of colour, and particularly Black women.[1]

Some of the external factors are personal to you, but are still things that you have no control over – these are things such as the financial education you had access to, your upbringing and also any health issues that might make it more difficult for you to develop and maintain a good relationship with money. A good example of this is the fact that certain mental illnesses, such as bipolar disorder, and neurodiversities like ADHD, can make money management materially more difficult for the people who experience them. Another is the way that your parents or guardians discussed money at home, and how exposed or shielded you were from the financial goings on in your childhood.

Of course, this is complicated by the fact that internal and external factors in financial wellbeing are also interdependent. They feed off one another, in ways both positive and negative. Encountering difficult financial situations or hardship can affect your confidence, self-worth and decision-making processes, which can then compound to create a toxic relationship with money that needs to be overcome. Meanwhile, developing inner resilience can have a positive effect on your external circumstances through the medium of your actions and being open to opportunities. This, in turn, can compound your fortunes in the opposite direction and help you to feel more confident and in control, which improves your relationship with money and often, also, your material financial situation.

Most of us will have a whole suite of systemic and personal factors, over which we have limited or no control, that affect our financial situation and relationship with money. It's important that we try to understand these, both to apply context to our actions in the past, and to make sure that our expectations of ourselves don't outweigh our resources.

What actually is financial wellbeing, and why should I care about mine?

Wellbeing, or wellness, is seen by many – especially those who are fond of expressions like 'snowflake' and 'woke' as insults, and view financial stability as a simple 'in vs out' equation – as a very current preoccupation. This makes sense in some ways – as the world has sped up, exposing us to more and more stressors, the need to focus on our own health and state of mind has increased. We need something to counterbalance the chaos of everyday life, the infinite channels of communication we are open to, and the wellness industry presents us with solutions that it claims will help us to achieve that elusive balance. But wellbeing runs much deeper than that, and psychologists and philosophers have been discussing and debating it for centuries, maybe even millennia. There is something fundamental about it, something that defies time and technology, but is rooted deeply inside of all of us. Wellbeing is, simply put, the business of feeling content and balanced in mind, body and soul, most of the time. It is not being in a constant good mood, but having the ability to cope well with life's inevitable ups and downs, to have a genuine resilience that doesn't rely on superficial things. For all of its simplicity in concept, it can be incredibly difficult in practice, and especially once you bring money into the equation.

One of those people spending their time mulling over what people need for general wellbeing was, perhaps, one of the most well-known psychologists in history: Abraham H.

Maslow. His 1943 paper, *A Theory of Human Motivation*,[2] in which he posed his ideas about what drives and fulfils us at the most fundamental level, has become one of the main ways that we understand wellbeing, but I have rarely, if ever, seen it applied to money. Maslow's theory or Hierarchy of Needs takes the form of a triangle or pyramid, with basic needs (physiological and safety) at the base, followed by psychological needs (belongingness, love and esteem), and then self-actualization needs at the very top. This can be really helpful in the way that we view privilege, because much of the wellness content we see on a day-to-day basis tends to focus on the top two sections of the pyramid, ignoring those critical needs at the base level.

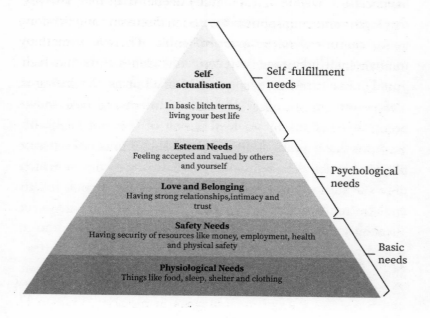

Self-actualisation

In basic bitch terms, living your best life

Self-fulfillment needs

Esteem Needs
Feeling accepted and valued by others and yourself

Love and Belonging
Having strong relationships,intimacy and trust

Psychological needs

Safety Needs
Having security of resources like money, employment, health and physical safety

Physiological Needs
Things like food, sleep, shelter and clothing

Basic needs

Maslow theorizes that the needs at the bottom of the pyramid must be satisfied before we can successfully fulfil those further up, which makes sense; but when I consider this pyramid, all I can think about is how closely linked money is to each and every one of the different levels. Even the most basic of our needs – food, water and rest – are impossible to meet without enough money to do so, and though the role of money changes as we move further down the hierarchy (or up the pyramid), its presence is constant. Money can dictate how safe and secure we feel, it can play a huge role in our intimate relationships, and it often acts as a measure of prestige and potential, both to ourselves and to others around us.

Seerut K. Chawla is a London-based integrative psychotherapist, whose insightful, human and utterly no-nonsense approach to wellbeing is absorbed by her 140k Instagram followers, including me (you can find her @seerutkchawla, if you'd like to experience her wisdom first hand). Her inclusive and realistic posts often present a challenging new viewpoint, and her Instagram feed is one of few mental health accounts that actually addresses the role that financial security plays in our ability to be mentally well. In one such post, which draws a line between the ideal resources for mental health and the fundamental ones, she writes, 'You can't go on a "healing journey" if you can't think straight because you're scared you won't be able to pay your rent or buy groceries.' She goes on to explain that *not* being able to focus your resources on 'healing' doesn't mean that something is wrong, only that most of this sort of wellness content is aimed at people who have the means to do so. She describes how striving to survive financially, and having to work hard just to keep the lights on, can be anxiety provoking and depressing, and that, 'sometimes you need therapy and sometimes you honestly just need more money/safe housing/job security/access to healthcare.'

For a long time, I've wondered why, when my experience of money is that it's so deeply emotional and affecting, money management and personal finance are still treated so clinically, and as though they are fair game for judgement and speculation. We've moved so far forward in terms of our understanding of mental wellbeing, but some of the deciding factors in how mentally healthy we feel – especially the less palatable ones, such as money – are still recoiled from. What I'd really like to see is a migration of personal finance from the business and economics sections of bookshops to the health and wellbeing ones, because I really didn't know what I was looking for until I stumbled across it – while recovering from financial difficulty – and I want more people to make the connection, sooner. Like many others, I was relying on the idea of some future utopia in which I was earning more, thinking that this would eventually and automatically trickle down through my life, improving my relationship with money and in turn making me feel better in general. That when I could afford to upgrade my lifestyle, I'd finally be happier, more fulfilled and less stressed.

Financial wellbeing is, I believe, the missing piece in the self-care puzzle. Accepting, acknowledging and understanding the role of money in all other areas of our lives is absolutely essential to living well – because money dictates so much of our lives to us, and has so much power over the way that we feel. It needs to be noted, too, that you don't have to be experiencing financial difficulty to want a better relationship with money. Even if you're earning enough to keep up with possibly toxic spending habits, or you're just about managing to get by, financial stress can keep you awake at night and play a part in feelings of discontent or low self-worth. It can cause arguments and ill-feeling, and make you feel resentful and envious – all of which are totally normal things to experience, but exhausting when they are constant or recurrent, especially if they are avoidable.

As with most things, because we are all individuals, with different priorities, circumstances, goals and experiences, each person is likely to have a slightly – or even wildly – different definition of financial wellbeing, and different ideas about what it would take for them to achieve it. What I value will inevitably be different from what you value, and we'll have different aims and aspirations for our lives, meaning that our ideas about what will make us feel fulfilled and content will be different too.

We also exist as part of a system, and care and wellbeing are systemic and collective responsibilities, as well as individual ones. So, making sure that we view our relationship with money in the context of society and the systems that we're trying to operate in is absolutely vital if we are to cultivate a sense of financial wellbeing in our lives. There is discomfort in knowing that what we would consider to be a small amount of money might be a huge sum to somebody else, and also that what we consider to be a huge amount of money might be completely insignificant to others, but we must be able to sit with that discomfort if we are going learn to manage our money in a calm and confident way.

Similar to many symbiotic relationships, the connection between general wellbeing and financial wellbeing is something of a chicken/egg-type situation. It's hard to work out exactly where to start making improvements, but the truth is that it's probably different for everyone. This book focuses on financial wellbeing, but you will find that there are some elements of each step that force you to think about and address things that might not seem money related. But because money is one of the most important currencies in our ability to thrive, and even survive, it is entwined in everything.

I'm confident that, when you follow these steps and prioritize your financial health, your general wellbeing will improve along with it. It will enable you to make choices to support your wellbeing and help you to thrive, safe in the knowledge that you and your money co-exist peacefully. That you are not unduly beholden to any creditor, employer or partner, and that you have the confidence to use your money as a tool to build a life that makes you happy.

Five Steps to Financial Wellbeing

One of the great privileges of having built a sizeable online community is that I have the opportunity to crowdsource information and opinions, and access to a whole host of different experiences and perspectives that enrich my knowledge and challenge my viewpoint. When I asked what financial wellbeing would mean for the people who engage with me on social media, the answers were simple and consistent:

'Feeling good about my money habits.'

'Not having to worry about affording food and petrol.'

'Earning money in a job that I don't loathe.'

'Not feeling scared and worried all the time.'

'Confidence that I fully understand my financial situation, for better or worse.'

'Feeling financially secure and satisfied with what I have.'

'Understanding my financial issues and being empowered to make good decisions.'

'Avoiding the monthly feast & famine cycle.'

'Not being afraid to spend my money even when I know I can afford it.'

None of these things should be too much to ask. When asked about financial wellbeing, almost nobody is aspiring to riches beyond their wildest dreams, or abundant material possessions – they just want to feel in control and at peace. Later in this book we will discuss the forces pushing us to aspire to material wealth rather than financial wellbeing, and how, if we don't have a solid idea ourselves of what a good relationship with money would look like, we risk never reaching a state of peace or contentment.

In recent months, I've seen 'financial wellbeing' co-opted by so many brands and publications as a way to repackage the same old advice that hasn't really been engaging or serving anyone for decades. This isn't that – or at least I really hope it isn't. Financial wellbeing is not a number or a percentage, as I've seen claimed in one Twitter thread, nor is it a certain budgeting technique or anything, really, that can be described in fewer than 280 characters. It is something deeply personal, constantly fluctuating and sometimes elusive. Something that requires at least, I don't know, 50,000 words or so to get to grips with. As glad as I am to see the concept firmly on the agenda, I'm keen to ensure that it's given its proper context and rightful place, because to lump it in with the 50-30-20 budgeting method is reductive and unhelpful. To suggest that there is one prescription that will treat any number of financial health issues is not helpful, because it's just not true. Your financial wellbeing is deeply personal and bespoke to you, and so it is up to you to figure out exactly what it looks like. This book will help you to do that.

Before we get into the five steps, I'd like you to take some time to think about what financial wellbeing would look like for you, because then you can shape the guidance throughout this book to suit your own need.

To give an example, for me financial wellbeing means:

- Feeling in control of the money that's coming in and out of my accounts.
- Not feeling anxious or worried about money (most of the time).
- Accepting and learning from my financial mistakes.
- Having the freedom to make decisions based on factors other than money.
- Knowing that I'm building a secure future for me and my children.

Before you read on, jot down a few bullet points and let them help you to create a framework for your own journey towards financial wellbeing. They can be as general or as tailored as you like, and you can change or add to them as you move through the steps.

Take it from someone who got it all wrong, and survived

For most of my adult life so far, my own sense of financial wellbeing was non-existent. I'd go so far as to say I was financially *unwell*, and it started more or less as soon as I started earning and spending my own money at eighteen. It followed me throughout university and into my first full-time job. I had my first son and got married young, and these big life milestones, coupled with a lack of understanding of what it meant to live within my means and some serious self-esteem issues, resulted in over £27,000 of credit card, overdraft and store card debt, which I finished paying off in early 2021. I chronicled this journey on my Instagram page, a warts-and-all account of what it was like to realize you had got things so wrong, and where I worked through the emotional and financial baggage that had enabled me to reach such a difficult and all-consuming situation. I asked myself why I had felt the need to spend lavishly on other people in order to feel reassured that they liked me, that I was worth something to them. Why I consistently ignored the warning signs in favour of daydreaming about a lottery win.

What I wasn't expecting on that day, when I finally reached breaking point and posted all of my credit card balances on the internet, was for it to resonate so much, with so many people. So many women, in particular. It was a strange feeling – a mixture of catharsis and sheer terror. I'd spent so long pretending that everything was fine, both on social media and to my friends and family, that this radical honesty about my failings was positively therapeutic. I wasn't ready to put my face to what seemed like such a huge sum of failings, so I remained anonymous for over a year, posting pink squares as

I chipped away at my debt. Then, as I started to apply more critical thought to my ideas about money and shame, and to talk more about letting go of those feelings of guilt, I realized that to remain anonymous for much longer could be perceived as hypocrisy. So, eventually, I dropped my cover and started talking about debt with my own face, voice and name.

Of course, my honesty about my money struggles also provoked some less empathetic responses, particularly around the time my first book was published, when the accompanying press campaign meant that my story was no longer confined to its sympathetic, and often empathetic, Instagram bubble. I watched myself reduced to my failings with money time and time again, the narratives of each of these stories focussing on all of my worst moments, my most regretful decisions. To a five-figure number that I had been trying to convince myself didn't define me. A lot of the shame that I had been working to diminish resurfaced and swallowed me whole. I wanted nothing more than to close my Instagram account and sink back into anonymity – for at least as long as it took me to regrow the skin that felt like it had been removed from me the moment that I dared to admit to something that so many other people experience. I saw commenters question my intelligence, the state of my marriage, my morality even, and it really, really hurt. It reminded me why I'd struggled to get help, or even to help myself, for so long in the first place. The urge to self-flagellate was strong, and I succumbed more than once to those feelings.

After a difficult, months-long vulnerability hangover, I realized that I didn't feel quite so raw anymore. My skin grew back, and it was thicker now. I felt ready to start challenging the moralizing of money and spending that had made me feel so awful, and to pull together an alternative narrative on money – one that helped people to understand their behaviour and make deeper changes, rather than attempting to shame or judge them into making superficial, punitive changes. It filled me with a new sense of purpose, and the stirrings of this book were born. I wanted to create something more than just a manual for using money – I wanted to teach people how to feel good about it. I wanted to create something that really explored the emotional and psychological side of money and health, rather than just paying lip service to it, or treating it as an irritating caveat to the usual prescriptive advice.

My relationship with money, though vastly improved from what it was, is still a work in progress, and most likely always will be. There will always be old habits that seem appealing when I'm at a low ebb, unfulfilled expectations that threaten my happiness, new temptations that try to divert my course. But learning to navigate these peaks and troughs without overwhelming anxiety or crushing despondency is at the very heart of true financial wellbeing. It's not a snapshot of a moment in time – an Instagram post holding the keys to your first home or a screenshot of those zero credit card balances – it's dynamic and ever-evolving. It's about all of the moments and experiences and decisions in between those snap-worthy events, where we want to live peacefully and confidently with our money. That's what I'm hoping to impart here – not a blow-by-blow account of how I did things, but a template for you to design a financial life that feels right for you.

I have made, and will probably continue to make, so many mistakes when it comes to money. The good news is that everybody else does too – they just won't always tell you about it. What's important to remember is that, in the same way that we only see one layer of anyone's life on social media, we are also very rarely privy to the inner workings of someone's bank account – even when we know them quite well. A good rule of thumb is to assume that even those you consider to be well-off, meticulously frugal or just really 'good with money' will have made at least one financial mistake. Mistakes are part of life, they are almost never completely irreparable and, even more importantly, they are an absolutely brilliant learning opportunity.

The missing piece in the self-care puzzle

As mentioned, I realized, once I pulled on the thread of what money meant to me, that personal finance has long occupied the wrong space on the bookshelves, the wrong section of the newspaper. It is lumped together with business and economics, the discussions too often led by a very specific type of person from a very specific type of background. With oodles of wealth privilege, and either no understanding – or an expired understanding – of what it means to find money difficult to understand or get to grips with. I didn't know where my messy finances fitted, because there was nowhere for them to go. There was a disconnect between what I knew in theory, and the decisions that I had been making in practice, and I couldn't find anybody talking about the solution to that. As I began to unravel things further, to understand them and to process them, I realized that there's a huge part of 'finance' that doesn't belong with bank accounts and credit scores at all. It belongs in the health and wellbeing space, along with all the other ways we look after ourselves. It is part of self-care – something that I find is increasingly reduced to or conflated with personal grooming or physical fitness – and a crucial part at that. There is so much more to self-care than the superficial or trend-led elements that we read about and feel compelled to try.

Money is often ignored in conversations about broader wellbeing; we are told to 'take a mental health day', 'treat yourself to a massage' or 'try this life-changing green juice' without any consideration that, for lots of people, even a day's worth of statutory sick pay will leave them short, and that medical prescriptions and nutritious food are enough of a financial strain for many. In addition to the monetary cost, these commercial solutions to being physically or emotionally unsettled will only paper over the cracks, if the reality is that your relationship with money is well and truly broken, and you are trying to quieten a feeling that comes from deeper down.

Alas, capitalism. The wellness industry is dripping in wealth privilege, and it's more convenient for brands to feign ignorance about the important role that money plays than to acknowledge and consider solutions for it. After all, are they not in it for . . . the money? It is very inconvenient for many businesses to acknowledge the fact that real self-care is not for sale. Somewhere in our busy lives we have lost the art of looking after ourselves, and tried to replace it with a scented candle and some CBD oil. That'll be £79, please.

At its very essence, self-care is found in the habits and rituals that we use to make sure that we are fulfilling those needs in Maslow's hierarchy, and a key element of that is to have a peaceful and purposeful relationship with money. So, financial wellbeing must be a consideration in how we look after ourselves, because when we lose control of that element of our lives, no amount of superficial grooming can make us feel okay.

Why is it so hard to talk about money – and why is it vital that we do?

It is not news to anybody that it's difficult to have an honest conversation about money. For everything that we are willing to admit to, there are a thousand things that go unsaid, because we are embarrassed or ashamed, or we don't think that people will understand. Internal shame is often mirrored by external judgement, whether directly or by proxy of a sensationalized newspaper headline, and we clam up. Sometimes we fear being berated, but sometimes we just don't want to be patronized. We certainly don't want to put ourselves in a position where our financial failings can be weaponized against us, so we don't say anything at all – even when it is bubbling violently just below the surface, robbing us of precious hours of sleep, limiting our choices and stunting our personal growth.

There are a few reasons why this is, I think, and each of them is quite complex and nuanced. It's not only down to personal fears and insecurities, but there are also broader societal issues that keep our lips sealed.

We're measuring ourselves by the wrong yardstick

Much of the narrative around money in society and the media is built around one single blueprint for how our financial lives should look – but it is a blueprint that is both out of date and out of touch with the reality in which most of us are now living. And yet we continue to measure our successes, and those of our peers, against an antiquated yardstick of early property ownership, jobs for life and affordable living costs. Not to mention the wedding and children we simply *must* have to make our lives complete. If we are female, we often feel as though we must also do this while looking a certain way – and all of that personal grooming and fast fashion comes at a financial cost too. This gold standard of money management – although unachievable for so many – circles us like an invisible bird of prey, threatening to peck our eyes out if we so much as think about buying an avocado or a takeaway coffee. This in turn makes it almost impossible to talk about money, especially if we feel like we're failing to live up to those standards or have different financial priorities.

So, we're caught between a rock and a hard place, and the more we don't talk about it – the more we keep hidden, the more we try to cover up – the harder it gets to talk about it. A vicious cycle that only ends in everyone feeling alone, even when we have so much of this stuff in common.

We don't want to be patronized

I find that there's an incorrect assumption among a lot of people that, just because you struggle with your relationship with money, you must also be terrible at maths, or ill-informed about personal finance, or both. While it's true that there's a correlation between financial confidence and financial literacy, being infantilized the moment that we mention money worries is not something that appeals to any of us. For people who have always got on just fine with their money, it can be difficult to understand how it feels to have a difficult relationship with it, and that can often manifest in a well-intentioned but hurtful or irritating lecture. There is, generally speaking, a lack of awareness of the connection between money and other factors, even for people who experience it themselves. There is a lightbulb moment for so many people when they realize that their money issues are rooted in other things, but it can be very frustrating to try to have a conversation with people who aren't quite there yet – or people who stubbornly refuse to accept it.

We're taught that it's not polite

The prickly fence around discussing money in a real, honest way is often put down to 'Britishness', but I'm not sure that that's always the case. It's true that, perhaps, in other cultures money is spoken about more openly, but I think there's still a lot that goes unsaid. With any discussion about money comes the inevitable associations of work, value and power, and that's not something anyone I've ever encountered seems to be comfortable with discussing at the pub. If we are squeamish about discussing money, it is for good reason. It's very difficult to talk about it in any meaningful way without venturing into unchartered territory, and peeling away the layers and complexities that underpin both our personal relationship with it and its role in our society can make things very uncomfortable very quickly.

As a society, we are quickly taught that broaching conversations that will inevitably lead to discomfort is not polite, and so we are conditioned towards small talk – which is fine in the office, or at a PTA barbecue, but these are things that we should be able to discuss with those close to us, at the very least. Yet these are the people that we often struggle most to confide in, because there is more at stake.

It messes with the power dynamic

Power dynamics in relationships fascinate me, and they are a topic in and of themselves, but what I have spent a long time paying particular attention to is how they are affected when money arises in conversation. Healthy interpersonal relationships usually have a power dynamic that is equal, or fairly close to equal as a baseline – and often we don't want to bring money into it, in case it alters things. This can, in turn, make our relationships more difficult to manage, or lead to awkwardness between friends or family members with different financial situations.

It's not only in our personal relationships that the money-power dynamic has an effect. I recently spoke as part of a panel on the topic of money and work, called 'Should you let your boss into your bank account?' One of the topics I was keen to table was the sensitivity of discussing money at work, because although the employer–employee relationship pivots on the fact that we all go to work in order to get paid, it's probably the place where we're least comfortable discussing personal finance issues. Having been through an awkward stage at a previous job, where the non-materialization of a promised pay rise made things even more difficult in my finances, I wanted to talk about the currents of power in those negotiations. To give away to your employer that you're struggling financially is a risky manoeuvre – not only in terms of potential embarrassment or awkwardness, but also because it involves giving away your most important bargaining chip as an employee. Realistically, if your employer knows that you're unlikely to take the financial risk of leaving your job, there's less pressure on them to progress your salary. You don't want them to know that they've got you.

In Step Two, we'll talk a little more about different types of power, how they relate to money, and how we can find a healthy way to navigate them, but for now, you might want to take some time to explore how this affects your own relationships, and note down any insights or realizations that you want to revisit later.

It feels good to talk

It's hard to deal with issues and overcome problems on our own, without a sounding board or shared knowledge. We'll discuss therapy in more detail a little later on, but there's a reason why talking therapies are prescribed or recommended to those going through a difficult time, or wrestling with something inside themselves. It feels good to talk. When we choke out our trauma or worries to someone with no vested interest in us being okay (obviously, your therapist wants to help you, but they don't rely on you for anything in their own lives), the shame loses a little of its purchase. The more that we talk about things, and learn to understand them, the more healthily we can process them. All of this applies as much to money, and our relationship with it, as to anything else. If we can break the chokehold that money often keeps us in, we can start to gain control over both the practical and the emotional side of our finances.

Feeling frozen in shame about financial mistakes that we have made, or knowledge and understanding that we lack, or a lack of financial privilege in our background, is often the thing that holds us back from seeking the information and support that we need. Money is one area where it is still not widely acceptable to be seen as vulnerable, so we build our walls high and dig our trenches deep, and we pretend that everything is fine, even when it's not. Because of this, sometimes even those people with significant financial privilege, in the form of wealthy (or even comfortably off) parents or access to good financial advice, will insist on struggling on alone, preferring the stress and anxiety to opening up or asking for help. As fortunate as it is to be in a position whereby you *could* ask for and receive financial help, the theoretical ability to seek support does not serve much of a purpose if financial shame and anxiety make it impossible to actually do so.

As well as the ability to access material help when needed, another thing that openness about money affords us is catharsis. Until I started spilling my darkest financial secrets to thousands of strangers, I was genuinely in the dark about how many other people struggled to manage their money, or had a complex relationship with their finances. For most of my adult life, I had genuinely assumed that the secret to being 'good with money' was something that everyone else had been imbibed with from an early age, that I was uniquely terrible at being an adult. Once I started talking about it, first in an anonymous confession on the internet, then more intimately with friends and family, I started to recognize the plethora of different ways in which a person can struggle with money, and just how common it is to do so.

The five steps

You might be asking how, after these last few pages, it's possible to narrow something so utterly enormous and complex as financial wellbeing down to five steps, and that is definitely a legitimate question. All of the themes and issues that we will cover here will bear further reflection and intro-spection, but these steps outline a framework that I believe to be fairly universal – one that I hope will make you feel included, supported and maybe even a little bit inspired. That is not to say that this is an exhaustive account of the actions that need to be taken to achieve a full sense of financial wellbeing, or a peaceful relationship with money, or that you will finish reading it and be 'fixed'. Like all good (I hope) personal develop-ment books, it needs to allow space for you to develop your own ideas and strategies for achieving this. If part of the problem with mainstream financial narratives is that they are too prescriptive, I certainly don't want to be complicit in that.

What these five steps will do is guide you to the places where you might have things to unpack, and give some structure to a journey that can often be difficult and confusing. They will give you scope to explore your own feelings and to connect the dots between what you do and how you feel; a jumping-off point to really get to the core of what is holding you back from achieving your financial goals, or making you feel anxious about money, or keeping you trapped in a cycle of emotional spending, or stopping you from achieving satisfaction no matter how much you earn or buy. If you dedicate yourself to completing each of these phases, are honest with yourself and open to the process, I promise that you will find it easier to navigate your relationship with money, to forgive yourself for slip-ups and to plan for a positive financial future.

For each step, there are exercises and methods that you can try in order to gain insight or reframe your thinking around money, because this is very much a 'doing' book as well as a reading book. It is certainly not a 'put it on a shelf and never look at it again' book; that won't help at all, and it's what we've all been used to doing with our finances instead of facing them head on. You might find that making notes and journaling your response to some of the questions and prompts throughout the five steps gives you something to really grab on to when you're looking to make changes, so that would always be my own personal recommendation, but it may not work for everyone.

The first couple of stages of this process involve getting to grips with the deeper, more mindset-based elements of your relationship with money, figuring out the role of money in your life and tweaking it so that you can put it in its rightful place. The later stages are more practical, but still with lots of mindset work, helping you to understand your current behaviours and thoughts in order to adapt them into more positive and helpful ones. It's a method that has really helped me reach a sense of peace and contentment with money, as well as driving material changes in the way I prioritize, spend, save and invest. I really hope and believe that it can help you too.

Step One
Overcoming your financial baggage

It's not really fair that the first step in the process is probably one of the hardest, but coming to terms with, and letting go of, your money mistakes is like laying the foundations of a house. It's not necessarily visible in the finished product, but skip it and your house will fall down – either immediately, or at some point in the future when you're least expecting it. In order for your new habits to properly take hold, you need to learn to understand your old ones, and identify anything that might sabotage your attempts to change them. There are many things that keep us locked in cycles of unwanted behaviour, and there's no evidence to suggest that it's possible to cut corners just because we're talking about something that can be measured in notes and coins.

Making peace with your mistakes is not only about habit change but self-forgiveness. Self-flagellation and shame are often defining factors in keeping us stuck in the same place, or even the same downward spiral. When we continue to define ourselves by mistakes that we have made in the past, we are telling ourselves that they could recur at any moment – and then, more often than not, they do. I've spoken to so many people who have pulled themselves from a difficult financial situation at great personal cost, only to end up in the same situation again a little while later – because they hadn't dealt with or accepted the factors that got them to that point in the first place. In fact, I too had also tried to fix the superficial problem without properly getting over the mistakes that I'd made, and it didn't work for me either. Any progress felt laboured, like I was pulling on a stiff elastic band, and I knew that it would need to spring back at some point. And then, of course, it always did, and I would find myself back at square one.

It's worth noting that this doesn't only apply to big financial mistakes. Sometimes it's only the smallest thing keeping us locked in those limiting beliefs about ourselves – that we're 'bad with money', that we 'just don't get it' etc. It might be the fact that you still have your student overdraft in your thirties, or that you once borrowed a fiver from a colleague and didn't pay it back, or that you were talked into an extortionate car finance arrangement on a brand new model when you were just looking for something to get you from A to B. It could be anything.

Before we get into this properly, I just want you to know that absolutely EVERYBODY makes mistakes with money, and if I'm honest, a large component in how big of a deal they are, or how ashamed we feel about them, is a little thing called wealth privilege. In other words, some people are just more comfortable with messing up with money than others, because their mistakes have less of an impact on their quality of life. Some people are able to brush off big errors of judgement with little afterthought because there is no risk to their base level of comfort and security, whereas others can make a small loss and feel floored by it. In other words, 'small' mistakes can feel catastrophic to some people, whereas wasting or losing quite a lot of money can feel quite small to others. This is usually due to external factors, but a key element in reducing shame and forgiving yourself on a deeper level is keeping things in context.

What can we learn from our financial mistakes?

- That we need to deal with underlying issues rather than just the symptoms.
- That it's not possible to out-earn a broken relationship with money.
- That openness about money is a critical part of our relationships.
- That there is power in vulnerability.
- That things aren't always as simple as they seem.
- That there are often other forces at play in our relationship with money.

Don't view your mistakes in isolation

I'd like you to think, for a moment, about reality TV. Imagine that you are in the editing room, watching things unfold. Access to a 24-hour loop of a whole medley of human behaviour – the good, the bad and the ugly. Now, imagine that your boss has told you that one person in this room must be painted as the villain, and that you need to cut out any provocations or situations that might make their actions understandable. Would that be fair?

Now, this is actually a well-documented phenomenon; lots of people have waltzed off reality TV shows expecting applause, only to be met with boos, thanks in part to their own behaviour but also because of all of the bits that *weren't* shown. The context that was edited out for dramatic effect, the unseen provocations and influences that led them to react in a particular way. We do ourselves a great disservice when we recreate that editing room in our own minds, cropping our mistakes right down to the action itself and removing any context or nuance, because the circumstances under which we make our decisions *matter*. They matter so much that it's not really possible to understand, and then correct, our behaviour without a comprehensive view of where we've gone wrong and why.

As much as some people are determined to conflate the two, reasons are not excuses. Accountability does not have to mean giving yourself a hard time in spite of difficult circumstances and being wilfully ignorant of the factors that contributed to your mistakes. Looking at and understanding the factors leading up to any money mistakes that you might have made does not equate to letting yourself off the hook entirely – it is about seeing what went wrong, so that you know what to do differently if that same set of circumstances occurs again. So that you can show yourself some compassion and understanding, in the same way that you would show both of those things to a close friend or family member who had made an error of judgement or slipped up in some way.

A lot of my spending issues reached a fever pitch while I was on maternity leave with my second son, in 2018. I look at some of the decisions that I made during that time – upping my credit limits, buying expensive, organic babygrows that he grew out of immediately, hiring a cleaner to come every other week even though we were struggling to make ends meet – and they seem ludicrous at first glance. I certainly found them difficult to forgive for quite a while. But when I switch to a broader lens and look at what was going on outside of those individual transactions, it becomes easier to see what was happening, and why. I was very lonely, exhausted and experiencing fairly all-consuming postnatal anxiety. The leap from one child to two was a shock to the system, and I felt as if I was drowning. When I remember how that felt, it's easier to cut myself a little bit of slack, and consider what I might do differently if we ever decide to have another child (unlikely – he's almost three now, and has slept through the night . . .

once). When doctors diagnose an illness, they don't just look at the individual symptoms to give them an idea of what's wrong and how to fix it – they look at how those symptoms relate to one another, what's exacerbating what. They ask you questions about your lifestyle – and if you've ever watched a medical drama, you'll know that some seemingly irrelevant aspect of the patient history almost always ends up being a critical detail. We really need to apply that context to our relationship with money if we want to figure out what went wrong, and what we can do to fix it.

Sometimes, we carry outdated ideas about our own ability to manage our money. Some financial mistakes come with a very long tail, meaning that even when your attitude and behaviour shift significantly in the intervening years, you can still be left dealing with the consequences of decisions that you made when you were much younger, and knew less about how things worked, or didn't have the perspective and life experience that you have now. It's really important to allow for growth in your money mindset, and dwelling on mistakes that you made years or sometimes even decades ago will keep you stuck in those limiting beliefs about your abilities.

Exercise: Identifying money mistakes

For the first exercise of this section, I'd like you to think about three money mistakes you've made. They might be big things, or smaller things, or absolutely minuscule things, but try to identify things that play on your mind, things that you often find yourself dwelling on. Then, expand the picture out. Look at where you were in your life, what you knew and didn't know. How you were feeling, how much you were earning – everything. Remember that this past version of you didn't have a crystal ball, and had no way of knowing what was lurking around the corner. You can do this in your head, of course, but you might find it a bit easier and more memorable if you do it on paper – it'll also help you a little later on.

Viewing your money mistakes in context is the first step towards forgiving yourself and moving on, which is a vital element of financial wellbeing. It will also help you to see past the shame and embarrassment to the *lesson*, that kernel of goodness right at the centre of the mistake or failure.

Challenge yourself to think about things differently

As you start to add context and explore the circumstances under which you made your mistakes, you might find yourself starting to consider things differently. That shame and self-loathing that you might have been feeling, the wince-inducing heat of the things you did wrong, might begin to fade as you start to become aware of your reasons for tripping up. The gut reaction for many people here, myself included, is to experience a bit of a guilt kick-back. When you start showing yourself some kindness and understanding, you might start to worry or feel guilty that you're giving yourself an easy ride, or letting yourself off too lightly. You might be concerned that letting go of the guilt and shame that you feel about the financial mistakes you've made will leave you open to making them again, but you need to trust me when I say that this isn't the case.

Of course, if your immediate response to any mistake is to shrug it off without a second thought, without even a moment of reflection, you will probably make it over and over again. You will continue doing the same thing, expecting different results – the very definition of insanity according to someone who almost certainly was not Albert Einstein (but he usually gets the credit in memes). Whoever said it, it makes sense. However, ignoring your mistakes is not the only way that this happens – it often occurs as the result of overanalysing and punishing yourself for your mistakes, or because you're waiting for some big moment of reckoning to set you on the right path. We need to find the sweet spot: accountability without unnecessary punishment. We need to acknowledge those mistakes in order to learn from them and move on, but overanalysing and dwelling on them will keep us locked in the same behaviours and deny us the space we need to grow.

Ways to stay accountable without self-flagellation

- Change your language – try to steer away from blame-based language and talk more about responsibility. For example, change 'I'm to blame for all of this financial stress' to 'It's my responsibility to resolve these financial issues'.
- Find a positive way of tracking your progress, and check in frequently.
- Don't tiptoe around things or shy away from the facts. Practise talking aloud about your finances, even if it's just in the mirror.
- Find like-minded people to talk about money with, and be honest with one another.
- Use a budgeting app that will warn you if you're spending a bit too much, and *heed its advice*.

Dealing with external judgement

As someone who is naturally very thin-skinned, I completely understand how much it hurts to be judged for having difficulties in your relationship with money, especially when those difficulties have manifested into something tangible and life-affecting, such as debt or an inability to save for your goals. We bear the weight of other people's judgements of us, or worse, the judgements that we *imagine* that they're making about us, like ankle weights. We might not always be overtly aware of them, but they make everything harder, slower and heavier. Fear of being judged for our actions with money can keep us paralyzed and unable to make decisions, while past instances of being judged or criticized can echo in our minds, cancelling out any and all positive feedback.

I'm going to let you in on a secret, though. You don't have to allow other people's judgements and opinions of you to affect you. They can knock on the door, they can huff and puff, but you do not have to let them in. Especially if those judgements come from people who don't really know you, or who have a completely different experience of life from you. You get to decide whose opinion matters to you, and whose advice you listen to – everything else is just superfluous, and you can learn to tune it out.

When I started to open up about my own relationship with money and the mistakes I'd made, I knew that I would be faced with other people's opinions of me and what I'd done. I knew that, for many people, the amount of debt that I'd managed to accrue was shocking, and I had to learn to not let that make me feel ashamed. We each have our own experience with money and attitudes towards it, and we each value different things – understanding this can help us to both minimize our judgements of others, and increase our own resilience to external judgements that we might face. We all make judgements about other people's behaviour when it doesn't align with our own set of values or priorities, whether we notice that we're doing it or not. Remember that the next time that you worry about someone judging you.

44

If you have enough conviction in your own way of doing things, and you feel steady and confident in your priorities, you'll feel better equipped to differentiate between good, helpful advice and somebody who may be applying their own belief system to your life, in a way that doesn't serve you.

Much of this is to do with having the right boundaries in place, which is something that we will talk about a little bit later, but while we're in this stage of understanding and making peace with your mistakes, try to remove any judgement or disappointment that you've experienced from the equation as you start to forgive yourself.

Self-forgiveness in practice

It's all very well acknowledging that we need to forgive ourselves for financial mistakes in order to move on from them, but I know better than most that it's easier said than done. When you're in the habit of dwelling on mistakes, and of tying every bit of unhappiness in your life now to a mistake that you made in the past, that place of genuine self-forgiveness might feel completely out of reach. There is also the fact that sometimes, when we make poor decisions with money, it has a knock-on effect on other people that we care about, and the guilt associated with that can be very valid. We'll talk about how to address that guilt and make amends, because it's an important part of moving on from your mistakes, but for now, let's focus on forgiving yourself.

The first thing that you need to do is to try to connect that bad feeling you're having to a particular event or decision. Sometime the threads connecting the actual act to the residual feeling can take a little while to trace – we don't always associate the fact that we feel anxious about money to that inheritance that we blew, or the fact that we're overspending on our children now to the fact that we couldn't afford to spoil them when they were younger etc. You can either work through all this in your head or journal it out, but it's hard to move forward in forgiving yourself if you can't actually pinpoint what you feel you did wrong.

The next step is to work out to what extent the mistake was your fault, using some of the insights you've gained from the early parts of this chapter. Consider why you made the choices that you made – were you an active participant, or were you passively allowing things to happen? Did you make those choices based on information that's different to the information available to you now? What were the external pressures involved?

Then, try to consider why you behaved that way. Can you access some of the thoughts and feelings that you were having at the time? Can you think about what mattered to you then, whether you were acting on a selfish impulse or trying to impress or please others?

Make sure that you're considering your mistakes from a place of compassion – try to suspend your judgement of yourself during this exercise. Remember that we all make mistakes, but ask yourself whether or not you knew that you were making the wrong choice at the time. For example, when I think about some of the spending decisions that I made when my relationship with money was at rock bottom, I recognize that I knew that I was creating problems for myself even as I was buying things – I just wasn't thinking of the longer-term consequences. I also see quite clearly now that I didn't feel that I was deserving of a good relationship with money and healthy finances, so many of my decisions were related to low self-esteem and a feeling of being undeserving. I also recognize that many more were due to a lack of patience and self-discipline, which enables me to identify areas that I might still need to work on, or at least watch out for. Forgiving yourself and knowing yourself – recognizing that you are flawed and a constant work-in-progress, as everybody is, go hand in hand.

Eventually, as you work through these mistakes, you will reach a point where you have to let it go. Guilt can be a useful emotion when it acts as a deterrent for repeating or participating in certain behaviours, but when we cling to it for too long, it can have the opposite effect. Remember to hold on to it only for as long as it's useful.

What did you learn?

Making mistakes can be painful, both during and after. But what we sometimes forget is that with every mistake there usually comes a lesson, and with lessons comes value. It's not possible to move through life without failing or erring in myriad ways, including financially – and even if there were, I'm not always sure that that's the path I'd choose. I know for a fact that my relationship with money is better now, having spent time and effort repairing it after a crisis, than it would have been had I not made some of those mistakes. I often feel that, had I not found myself in a situation whereby I was forced to deal with my mistakes head on or else face financial ruin, I might have chugged through life constantly living a little bit beyond my means, never planning for the future, always a little bit anxious about money. I might never have learned to be proactive in looking after my financial wellbeing. The lessons we learn from making mistakes with money are as valuable as actual cash, but only if we learn to see them that way. If we allow them to become embedded into our souls, if we allow them to undermine our confidence, then they become a self-fulfilling prophecy; a never-ending cycle of errors, blame and shame.

Exercise: Lessons from your money mistakes

Take the three mistakes you jotted down earlier, and take some time to think about what they taught you. There will likely be some practical things, based on an underlying lack of financial literacy or education at the time, but there could also be some deeper learnings about your relationship with money and your financial habits.

Guilt and apologies

Sometimes we make mistakes with money that hurt other people. We borrow it from people we care about but can't or don't pay it back, we hide financial worries from a partner, we make promises that we can't keep. And, while this chapter is heavily focussed on self-forgiveness and overcoming the shame and guilt that accompany financial mistakes, it would be remiss of me to ignore the hurt feelings of those people; firstly, because they are important in their own right, and, secondly, because *you* won't be able to forget them. If there are people who you care about, who you have hurt in some way that relates to money, you will probably struggle to find any real sense of financial wellbeing until you have made amends.

It takes courage to apologize, especially when the issue is something that's as awkward to talk about as money. It's likely that the other person or people don't feel able to bring up the hurt, because confrontation is something that most of us struggle with anyway, and when you pair that with our cultural resistance to talking about money, it's a recipe for brewing resentment and awkwardness. They might also be worrying about putting extra pressure on you if they're aware of any money worries that you're having, which can create a painful cocktail of conflicting emotions for them. I have spoken to countless people on both sides of the equation, and I've been in both situations myself. It's painful to be either person in the situation, but if you're the one who's done the hurting, no matter how unintentional, no matter how much you were also hurting yourself at the same time, it is up to you to be the one to make amends. I promise, you'll feel better for it.

There is a reason why 'making amends' comes later on in the various programmes that people use for getting back on track when their life has taken a rogue turn.[1] It takes strength and resilience to face the fact that our actions affect people other than ourselves, and when you are still at the very early, vulnerable stages of self-forgiveness, that strength and resilience might not yet be reliable, or even present at all. So, when you're ready, here are a few ways that you can look at broaching the conversation:

- Meet the person in a neutral place. A walk is always nice – I always find difficult conversations flow easier when there's some movement involved, and fresh air is often a bit of an antidote to anxiety.
- Don't beat around the bush. Your intention with this conversation is to apologize, and the longer you draw it out, the more difficult it will be. A good opening line is 'I want to talk to you about the time when I did X. It was wrong of me, and I owe you an apology. I'm really sorry.'

- Giving reasons might feel important to you, and it might help to give the other person some much-needed context, which can actually help to reduce the hurt that they are feeling. However, it's important not to drag these out too much, because then you risk making this apology all about you, and you might start to invalidate the other person's feelings without meaning to. Simply briefly explain the circumstances surrounding the mistake, and reassure the other person that your actions weren't a reflection of how much you value them.

- Where there are actual amends to be made, in the form of money that needs to be paid back or trust that needs to be rebuilt, make sure that you enter the conversation with a plan for that. You can then propose this to the other person – but bear in mind that it's up to them whether or not they accept it.

Most people really appreciate a sincere apology, and most people also realize that money can be a tricky topic to discuss. Just remember that the other person doesn't have to accept your apology or forgive you, and that this shouldn't be your motivation for apologizing to them. You're not trying to achieve absolution, you are trying to express how sorry you are. Despite the fact that you're taking this step in pursuit of your own sense of financial wellbeing, this part is not really for you, it's for them.

A catalogue of money mistakes

We all know that there's catharsis and comfort in knowing that we're not alone in our struggles and errors, and so that's what I want to offer to you to help you to move forward with this first step. One of the biggest components that I found was keeping me locked in that horrible feeling of shame and despair, solidifying that self-diagnosis of myself as hopeless with money, was feeling that I was alone in my mistakes. Knowing that I wasn't, and seeing people I liked and respected, people in a huge variety of situations and from a huge variety of different backgrounds, admitting to experiencing the same challenges as me was a huge catalyst for change.

When I deliver workplace talks or consultations, the first exercise that I do with participants is to ask them to think of three mistakes they've made with money, big or small. I then encourage them to share with the group – and one of two things will happen. Rarely, people keep their cards very close to their chest and there is little to no activity – understandable, as work can be a very difficult place to be vulnerable – but what usually happens is that one person is brave enough to go first, and then the dominoes fall. People talk about money that they lent and never got back, money that they wasted, credit card balances that they regret and everything in between, and it feels like there is a collective sigh of relief. The more people reveal, the better everyone feels, and the happier they are to discuss their own relationship with money, in a sort of positive snowball effect.

So, I thought I would crowdsource some catharsis for you as part of this step, because it's much easier to open yourself up to facing and forgiving your financial mistakes when you know others are right there with you. Here are a few that come up repeatedly in my conversations with people – on social media, in workshops, and in real life:

- Lending money to family, friends or ex-partners.
- Borrowing money from friends and family and not being able to afford to pay it back.
- Borrowing from savings to cover monthly outgoings and never putting it back.
- Getting a credit card as soon as they turned eighteen, not really knowing how to manage them.
- Defaulting on bills that went to the wrong address.
- Not paying fines on time and allowing fees to spiral.
- Not cancelling credit cards after they're paid off.
- Blowing a large inheritance.
- Spending to try to keep up with others.
- Relying on credit cards and not being real about what they could afford.
- Taking a consolidation loan to pay off credit cards, then maxing them out again.
- Never checking their bank account.
- Not thinking about the future.
- Not starting to save sooner.

These are all mistakes that completely normal, functioning adults make all the time, and this is just a small fraction of a more comprehensive list. Just because nobody is telling you directly about the mistakes that they're making, doesn't mean it's not happening. Especially in the UK, we have a tendency to pretend that everything is fine while we're struggling under the surface, and we see being 'good with money' as a key component of successful adulthood. To admit to failings is to admit that we are still, in some ways, a little more juvenile than we pretend to be – and people rarely want to concede that they're not quite there yet.

Mistake-sharing can be such a cathartic and soothing exercise, reducing shame and helping you to break through the barriers that are stopping you from finding solutions.

Learning to trust yourself again

As I've said, struggling to find financial wellbeing doesn't always mean that you've made catastrophic mistakes with money, or that you're experiencing financial difficulty, but it does mean that there's some kind of discord in your relationship with money that is affecting the way that you use it. You might be quite new to managing your personal finances, or have a few years under your belt, and everyone's experiences with money are different. But if you've made mistakes with money, you might find it difficult to trust yourself in the future, especially as successfully managing your finances means making hundreds of decisions, big and small, all the time. In order to achieve financial wellbeing, we have to be comfortable making those decisions, and learn to trust our own judgement even when we know that it's led us astray before – and that can be really hard to do.

When I finished paying off the personal debt that forced me to confront my relationship with money, it coincided with some really lucrative opportunities, which meant that I was earning more than I had ever done before. For such a long time I'd had this one main goal, one main purpose – fixing my past mistakes and paying off my credit cards. It had been more or less my sole focus, and while I'd found a path to financial wellbeing for the duration of that journey, suddenly having more money and no debt to pay off was both exhilarating and terrifying. Even though I knew that I had successfully managed to transform my relationship with money in so many ways, I worried about whether my commitment to healthier finances would waver now I'd achieved that goal, and being responsible for more money made me nervous. What if I made those same mistakes again? After all, we all know that simply earning or inheriting more money doesn't automatically fix your relationship with it.

I realized that I needed to learn to better trust my own judgement, and to trust the changes that I had made. I looked back over the previous two years, thinking about mistakes I had made in the past, and asking myself whether I'd make those same errors of judgment again. I realized that no, I wouldn't. I saw clearly, perhaps for the first time, how much had changed, from the external circumstances that dictated my options to the way that I now prioritized things, and the forces that I was now wise to. I realized that I had far more knowledge, and my automatic responses to things were different, that I was making better, more positive decisions without even really trying.

That is what I'd like you to do, as the concluding part of this first, difficult but necessary step. I'd like you to begin the process of learning to trust yourself again. You can't just opt out of earning and spending money in everyday life, and you can't achieve financial wellbeing if you're constantly second-guessing every decision.

There are lots of suggested ways for people to rediscover their gut instinct – that strong feeling that's supposed to tell us what to do whenever we need to make a choice, but in my experience, what you actually need to try to do is turn down the volume on all of the other voices vying for your attention in order to be able to actually hear yourself. In the digital age, an age where we're exposed to tens of thousands of different opinions and viewpoints every time we go online, where we are chased around the internet by brands clamouring to tell us why we *need* their product, those other voices can be so loud that our own instincts are reduced to the tiniest squeak. We're so preoccupied by what others are doing, what others think we should be doing, that we become disconnected from our own internal compass and lose sight of our own priorities. If we can't hear ourselves think, how can we even contemplate trusting ourselves? In her memoir, *Untamed*, Glennon Doyle calls this feeling, this absolute certainty deep inside, 'the knowing',[2] and explains that she discovered it by just shutting herself inside a cupboard until the only voice left in her head was her own. Every cupboard in my home is stuffed to the brim with all kinds of crap, and I'd rather not be crushed by an avalanche of old baby clothes and emergency chairs in the pursuit of knowing myself, but I have found meditation to be really helpful when it comes to learning to trust my gut and weeding out unwanted distractions.

When your brain is constantly whirring at a hundred miles per hour, the thought of achieving any kind of meditative state instead of doing something more *active*, especially when you're used to thinking of money in such purely practical terms, might seem counterproductive. But readying the ground for better financial confidence and clearer, quicker decision-making will save you a lot of time and uncertainty later on.

Meditation and mindfulness are not things that come naturally to me, nor to anybody else that I know. I suppose if we all found it easy to clear our minds, we probably wouldn't need to practise meditation in the first place. The most unlikely people are probably the ones who need it the most – just think about Don Draper in *Mad Men* and that final shot of him, eyes closed, tension finally released just a little. Sometimes these practices can feel a little bit silly or alien, especially if we're doing them in pursuit of something as practical and seemingly unrelated as better money management, but remember that confidence in your ability to make the right decisions is absolutely essential to a good relationship with money. Allow yourself to be open to this and it will pay dividends, maybe literally.

There are lots of ways to access meditation, from practising by yourself to guided classes and apps. It can be quite difficult to find the discipline or space needed to just start meditating on your own, especially if you don't have access to a cupboard like Glennon Doyle's, but the market for mindfulness tools is booming. Apps such as Headspace and Calm are well established and well-loved – *Open Up* author Alex Holder even has a Mindful Money course on Headspace – while the Clementine hypnotherapy app has courses to help reduce internal chatter and soothe self-doubt. Meanwhile, guided meditation can be accessed in person or digitally via lots of different channels – check what's available in your local authority. If you'd like to give it a go yourself, here are a couple of meditation exercises you can do to get started – just bear in mind that it might take a little while to access that state, and be patient.

A meditation exercise for self-trust

1. Find a safe, quiet space, and make sure you're comfortable. You can sit, stand or lie down – whatever feels good for you.
2. Close your eyes if that feels okay – otherwise you can practise a 'soft gaze', where you look ahead but allow

your vision to slide out of focus, so that you're not looking at one particular spot.

3. Focus on your breath, but just allow it to be as it is. Don't actively try to deepen it or slow it down artificially – you'll probably find that this happens naturally as you start to relax.

4. When you feel things start to settle, place either one or both of your hands on your heart or belly. This will allow you to feel more centred in yourself, which is a key element of self-trust.

5. Now, gently bring to mind a situation in which you feel that you might need guidance. It's probably best not to start with a huge, life-changing decision, rather something a little bit easier, and with lower stakes.

6. One by one, imagine the different actions that you could take, and explore the things that you feel when you bring each one to mind. You might have a strong emotional reaction in one direction or another, or you might feel nothing.

7. If you feel nothing for a particular option, this is probably an indicator to let that option go.

8. Strong feelings might take a longer time to decipher, but you will likely feel your consciousness push you in a particular direction. Take some time to ponder each of these options in a non-judgemental way until you start to feel a sense of certainty.

9. When you hit upon something solid, be aware of your breathing and how you feel. Just because something is the right decision for you, doesn't mean that it's an easy one. But remember that we can all do hard things.

10. Close your practice with a feeling of gratitude – to yourself for setting aside the time to meditate, and to your consciousness for guiding you in making this decision.

The more that you do this, the quicker you'll be able to access that certainty in daily life without having to slip into your meditative state. When you strengthen your decision-making muscles, you make it easier to trust yourself.

As well as the work that you do internally to discover and trust your own judgement, you also need to start putting that decisiveness into practice – even if you have to 'fake it 'til you make it'. Practise asserting yourself with people that you trust, and see how it feels to put your own financial wellbeing first in situations where there's a choice between what's easy and what's right for you. We'll talk about this more in Step Two, where we explore the relationship between people-pleasing and financial wellbeing.

Is your financial past keeping you stuck?

Sometimes – perhaps even often – there is an element of trauma, or at least pain, to our financial past that keeps us stuck in certain behaviours that affect our relationship with money. For most of us, this starts with the environment we grew up in – whether there was enough money, whether money was spoken about, whether it was used to buy our affection or compensate for missed time, whether our parents passed on any degree of financial education whatsoever. For most of us, by the time we start earning and managing our own money, we have some sort of relationship with it already, whether we were aware of it or not. This, then, has an opportunity to compound throughout our young adulthood, as we shuffle ourselves into categories – 'I'm a real over spender' or 'Oh, everyone hates me down the pub, I'm really tight'.

It might help, in understanding your current financial situation and relationship with money, to think about some of those early experiences with it and try to slot them into place. A feeling that money is scarcer or more abundant than it actually is, and what we define as a lot or a little money probably dates back to our childhood, and if we can start to unpick those attitudes and perceptions, we often spark life-changing revelations. We might also remember certain events that taught us to perceive money in a certain way, or to attach a certain feeling to it – for example, I very clearly remember, when our household finances were in disarray during my teenage years, several visits to the supermarket where our debit card was declined. How upset and embarrassed my mum was, the second-hand shame that I felt – and would go on to feel first-hand when the same thing happened to me a few years later. It's an odd phenomenon, the way that sometimes we recoil from our parents' mistakes, marching resolutely in the opposite direction, and sometimes we seem destined to repeat them. Our brains don't always seem to take the most logical route, and understanding how our past shapes our current attitude to money can take a little more unpacking – but it's important that we try to unravel this thread and unearth these experiences that could be holding us back or keeping us locked in a mindset that's preventing us from achieving a sense of financial wellbeing.

I spoke to Lydia,* who has linked what she describes as a hatred of money to feeling unworthy as a child. 'I have worked out that my overspending is really a wish to get rid of money in my account, like it's "dirty",' she says. 'My Dad used to "buy our love" with money and gifts that we didn't want. I hated money as a child, and I hate it now – how it makes me feel, how people act around it and how people use it as a power play. I'm now trying to work through this with my therapist.'

How our relationship with money can change throughout our lives, and in response to our relationships, is something that is

---

* I have changed all names to preserve anonymity.

always worth exploring when we're looking for answers about how to move forward. When we choose a partner, we so rarely consider financial compatibility – and it's easy to see why, as it's not exactly the sexiest or most romantic topic in the world – but who we share our lives with has a huge impact on our relationship with money.

Charlotte* explains how she started off with a positive relationship with money, working to earn it from a young age and planning for her future. 'Growing up, from the age of fourteen, I worked for my money – school holidays, weekends, evenings . . . you name it, I worked it. I don't remember saving any of this money in my teenage years, but I do remember that any money I was gifted for Christmas or birthdays, half of it went into my bank account, which contributed to my ability to buy a car at eighteen. I left university after three months, deciding it wasn't for me, and began working full time. This is when I started to save regularly, through a financial adviser, into a stocks and shares ISA and a pension.'

Charlotte's money habits changed, though, when she met her ex-partner. 'We used all of my savings as a deposit to buy a house together, when I was twenty-one,' she says. 'He was a builder and worked for cash in hand, while my salary went into the bank to cover the bills. Except we didn't have individual accounts, we just had one account between us for bills and living expenses, and he had access to my salary, but I never had access to his cash. He would regularly drain the account, took out an overdraft to cover the bills, and basically taught

63

me to live off credit because, in his words, "that's what it is there for – what's the point of having it otherwise?" We didn't have a penny of savings between us, having (thankfully) forgotten about my ISA by this point. When a debt collector turned up because of an accident my partner had had, which I knew nothing about, my parents had to bail us out. They did this more times than I care to remember.'

Since splitting from her partner, it's been a rocky path to recovery for Charlotte, but she's getting there. 'Once we had split up and sold the house, I finally had some savings again, but I also had a new-born baby and no child support to claim. I was still living in this cycle of living in debt and maxing out credit on cards, store accounts – you name it, I had it.

'I was able to clear some of it using my forgotten ISA, but the cycle just continued. By the time it got really out of control, I had used all the savings I had from the ISA and the house sale, and I was back at maximum balances. My parents would clear it all off, I would set up a standing order to pay them back, and start the cycle all over again. At one point I was receiving so much mail that my mother, who I lived with, googled the addresses on the back of the envelopes, and quickly worked out the problem without having to open the letters.

'Not until I was twenty-nine did I realize that I had to stop this. I didn't want to be thirty and living with my parents, with my own child. Only since the pandemic have I become completely debt free. I've been fortunate to have been able to do my job from home and reduce my outgoings considerably, paying off any and all remaining balances.

'I still live with my parents, but I now have a plan to own my own home. I have a PowerPoint presentation and everything.'

Charlotte's story can be typical of how our experiences with money can shape our attitude and behaviour with it, and how difficult those cycles can be to break – but it is also an example of what's possible once you start to understand and process those behaviours.

Important to note: The role of money in relationships can be as simple as having different attitudes to spending and saving, but it can also wander into the realms of financial abuse, which the organisation Women's Aid defines as '[abuse which] involves a perpetrator using or misusing money which limits and controls their partner's current and future actions and their freedom of choice. It can include using credit cards without permission, putting contractual obligations in their partner's name, and gambling with family assets.'[3] The lines when it comes to financial abuse can be blurry, and it can feel difficult to define, but it's important to address any behaviour that might be moving into this territory, because control of resources, including money, can be a barrier to leaving a relationship that is abusive in other ways too.

Laura* has a similarly complex relationship with money, this time stemming from feeling financially insecure as a child.

Her father moved jobs a lot when she was young, leading to them moving house frequently too, and she can remember being aware that money was very tight from the age of four or five years old. 'Dad didn't hold down jobs for long,' she says, 'so even when money was coming in, it never felt secure. My dad was always quite generous with money – when he had it, it was for spending, whereas my mum was much more sensible. I remember when we got some money from an employment tribunal and my dad treated me to two new dresses. Even then, aged eight or nine, I can remember thinking that it would have been better to put it away for a rainy day.'

Laura's parents divorced when she was twelve, and the money worries got worse, with her mum working three jobs to make ends meet, no child maintenance payments, and having to remortgage the house. 'I started working as soon as I could, and did as many hours as I could physically manage,' she says. 'My choice of university was based on affordability and, again, I worked long hours throughout but ended up with debt. This continued into my first few years of work. I felt like I was earning a decent wage – I started on £26.5k – and so should be able to keep up with all my colleagues. At that time, I didn't realize that they were all still being funded by the bank of mum and dad in one way or another.'

This issue with comparison and keeping up with those who – whether we realize it or not – have greater financial means than us is something that comes up often in my conversations about money. When we are thrown together with other people from different backgrounds, and especially when circumstances conspire to change our social sphere, whether that's at university, at work or at the school gates, it's all too easy to assume that everyone else is working with the same resources that we are. After a while, Laura realized that if she wanted to feel financially secure and comfortable, she would need to focus on paying off debt and starting to save, rather than spending to keep up with her colleagues. A positive choice in itself, but Laura says that it didn't solve her money anxiety. 'Once I started to have savings, I realized how precarious my previous position was and became obsessed with having a safety net,' she says. 'This feeling has never really gone away. I constantly think about how much money is in the bank.

'About five years ago, I burned out in my £80,000 per year corporate job and left without another to go to,' Laura reveals. 'This was terrifying, despite having about £20,000 in the bank at the time. I'm now contracting, and started on a rate of £700 a day, which is now £1,100 a day. My husband and I have around £200,000 in savings and no mortgage, but we're not doing much with it – mostly out of fear that we might make a mistake.'

I look at Laura's material situation – as you may too – and think that, on paper, it looks absolutely ideal. You might imagine that a person with that level of income and financial safety net would feel secure, but Laura still doesn't. 'I still feel sick at the thought of an unexpected expense, even though we'd have plenty of cash to cover a new boiler or whatever,' she says. 'As kids, when something went wrong with the house or the car, the panic was real. I still run through disaster situations in my head about how things might go wrong, and I can't afford to fix it.'

Most of us have heard, in some way or another, of body dysmorphia: people whose image in the mirror is distorted in some way or another, which gives them a warped and difficult relationship with their body. In an episode of the fantastic In Good Company[4] podcast, host Otegha Uwagba talks to her guest, artist and data journalist Mona Chalabi, about 'money dysmorphia' – the idea that experiences from our past can colour our relationship with money so deeply that we stop being able to tell what the real lay of the land actually is. This dissonance means that it's possible to know, logically, that you can afford something, but that there is always a voice telling you that you might need that money for something else – that there might still not be enough. Chalabi also wrote an article about this for the *Guardian* in 2019, entitled: 'Why I can't let myself have nice things'.[5] Chalabi writes that she is unable to recognise the fact that she has money, even though she knows objectively that this is the case. She describes hesitating to order an expensive burger in a restaurant, even though she knows she can comfortably do so. 'But still,' she writes, 'I'll sit at the table stewing with anxiety over what I might need that money for someday. My warped reality comes from fears about the future – one where I might be back in a dingy bedsit, unable to pay bills or, even worse, relying on a man.'

I discussed this with my husband, who grew up in a household where money was always very tight – though he always had everything he needed, he had an awareness of the scarcity of money and the need to work in order to earn it from a very early age. He described to me how spending anything above £30 tends to make him anxious, even now that he has a decent disposable income and no debt, and how any purchase above that amount makes him feel immediately guilty, even when it's a necessary one. This leads to a reluctance to spend any money at all from his personal account for at least a few days afterward. He finds it easier with our joint account, he says, because the responsibility for what goes in and out of that account is shared, and not all on his shoulders.

Conversely, with money dysmorphia, you might be aware that you really can't afford something – that the money in your account is spoken for already, or that your credit card balance is starting to scare you – but something pushes you to see it as free cash. This, quite opposite, experience is the one that I relate to personally. Looking back, I can see that I was painfully optimistic about my financial prospects, even when things were going very badly indeed. This optimism stemmed, perhaps, from the fact that I had never really been made to feel the impact of making poor financial decisions, and had been shielded from the financial difficulties faced by my family when I was a child. There was always enough of a safety net or a bailout that I was able to rest on my laurels, and it made for a really rude awakening when I reached that breaking point, where there was no money left and I was panicking about how to pay my rent. All the while that I was moving small amounts of money from one account to another, trying to plug the ever-growing holes in my budget, I was also, somehow, thinking about which new rug would look nicest in our living room.

It's a distraction, of course, from the real situation – a form of burying one's head in the sand in order to ward off that scary acknowledgement that things might not be under your control. If there is money for a new rug, then how can there possibly be a problem? La la la, I'm not listening.

Maria* has also experienced this sort of money dysmorphia: 'I was totally in denial,' she says, 'I suppose I thought that I could juggle it and was okay as long as I had a wage coming in to pay the debt. Then, Covid hit, and I no longer had a wage – only then did I face up to things. I used to do things to try and keep up with friends, like nights out and holidays, and I'm also a single mum and have never wanted my daughter to miss out, so I always felt that I needed to get her the best of the best – clubs, extra-curricular activities etc.'

The research that Mona Chalabi references in her *Guardian* piece, a study entitled, 'The relationship between objective and subjective wealth is moderated by financial control and mediated by money anxiety', published in the *Journal of Economic Psychology* in 2014,[6] discusses the relationship between objective and subjective wealth – i.e. how much money we have vs how much money we think we have – and identifies money anxiety as one of the key influencers of a disconnect between the two. It also shows that there is a closer correlation between objective and subjective wealth – i.e. less risk of money dysmorphia – in people who have a high level of financial control and planning. These findings really hold true to the experiences that I've encountered, and is why developing a stronger connection to our finances, and forming rituals and habits around practices such as budgeting, are the red threads running through these five steps.

Exercise: Unpacking your financial past

This is a journaling exercise, and it could take a little while. Try to clear some space in your day, and sit in the calmest environment that you can find, then give yourself a blank piece of paper or a fresh page in a notebook. As you reflect on the topics raised in this section, I'd like you to think about how your own attitude towards money has been formed, and see if you can link anything together. You'll probably realize fairly quickly that any unhealthy elements in your relationship with money have been sparked by something in your past. As you journal this out, see if you can draw lines and arrows connecting them together. You might then want to summarize on a separate page, giving you a sort of guide to understanding your own behaviour around money – which will, in turn, give you the key to unlocking a better relationship with your finances.

Financial therapy – a gap in the market?

When our financial past can be so complicated, and so intertwined with our relationships and experiences from a very young age, it makes sense that we might need some help to dissect our feelings about it and move on from any related trauma. Especially because, as is evidenced by almost every person I've spoken to about money, these learned responses, fears, anxieties and coping mechanisms may actually be sabotaging all of our attempts to have a peaceful, controlled and more *neutral* relationship with money in the present. When our judgement is clouded by our complicated feelings about money, it becomes far more difficult to make the informed and positive decisions that will lead us to a better financial future, or even to be able to enjoy the money that we have earned. Financial therapists do, in fact, exist, though they seem to be more established in America than in the UK. The practice couples traditional financial advice with an exploration of the psychological blocks and issues that shape our relationship with money, though the depth of financial advice that therapists, who usually come from a psychology or mental health background, are able to give varies. As an emerging practice, there are obviously wrinkles to be ironed out and barriers to be overcome – one of these being that seeing a professional trained in both fields comes with a financial cost, which may be counter-intuitive for some. It comes down to the age-old question of whether an initial financial investment will pay dividends in the future and, as with all therapy, it's not a magical solution.

Financial therapy has yet to make its way to the UK mainstream, but financial coaching – a softer practice that explores some of the emotional elements of money – is growing in popularity. For a 2016 *Guardian* piece, journalist Nione Meakin spoke to financial coach Simonne Gnessen about her difficulties in managing her finances, writing: 'Talking about money with a stranger feels both exposing and liberating. It's a subject that provokes strong emotions, but we rarely discuss it even with our closest friends. Perhaps financial therapy just offers a much-needed platform to discuss these feelings with someone who won't judge us.' She concludes that, for her, looking into these underlying feelings and associations is interesting, but that it becomes useful when patterns of harmful behaviour are uncovered, especially as we tend to repeat mistakes that we make in other areas of our lives.[7]

Ellie Austin-Williams is a financial coach, and trained under Simonne Gnessen to get her certification. She works with people to help them to understand their relationship with money better, and to overcome some of the behaviours that might be sabotaging their financial wellbeing.

'There's such an advice gap when it comes to money,' she says. 'Traditional financial advice serves so few people, and it's hugely product focussed. It's not about education, because a financial advisor will take action on behalf of their client. The business model of financial advice means that it's not worth a financial advisor's time to advise people controlling a regular amount of money. The people who are served are the people who already have wealth to manage, as opposed to people who are looking to manage their money better and build a comfortable level of wealth from scratch.

'So, we need something to bridge that advice gap, and that is where financial coaching comes in. Most people have had no financial education, and have just picked up bank accounts, credit cards and financial habits almost by osmosis as they've grown up. They don't have the information that they need to make informed and considered decisions. Coaching is a lot about the emotions, and helping people to ask themselves the questions that they need to ask themselves about how they relate to money – it's not about solving problems for them, but giving them the tools and information to solve those problems themselves. People need and want guidance – a clear path to follow, rather than having to cruise the internet looking for answers.'

I asked her about the most common issues that she sees as a financial coach, and she told me, 'It's mostly really simple things. Most people need help and support to organize and manage their finances on a practical level. It might be that their circumstances have changed – that they're single and have just changed income, or a couple who've just moved in together etc – and they need to recalibrate, or that they're a bit stuck trying to work towards their goals. Some people just don't know where to start. For others it's about identifying what their spending triggers are, and what's causing them to struggle with their emotions when it comes to money. The most common things are people who either overspend or struggle to spend anything at all.'

Ellie's simplest tip for anyone wanting to address their relationship with money is just to get started. 'Don't expect it to be a quick process. Understanding, evaluating and shifting your relationship with money can be a long process. A lot of people don't want to start because they think it will be too hard, or they expect everything to slot into place really quickly and give up when it doesn't. The key is just sitting down with yourself and addressing where you are right now, both emotionally and practically. Look at the big picture, collect all of the information and then you'll be in the best position to start making changes.'

It can be very difficult to open up about money, even to someone who we're paying to help us to work through our problems, but we do absolutely *have* to talk about it in order to break that barrier, that feeling of taboo that keeps us locked in unhelpful cycles of shame and regret. Therapy is supposed to be a safe space for us to discuss whatever is bothering us, to resolve issues from our pasts and forgive ourselves for our mistakes, and we absolutely should be able to talk about money in that space. Given the complexity of the role that money plays in our lives, and how many other issues it affects and is affected by, it's puzzling to think that 'financial therapy' is not a thing in the same way that 'couples therapy' is. In my view, there is a gap in the market for professional therapists with a thorough understanding of money, who would be able to offer a holistic approach to personal finance, as well as helping clients to heal the wounds left by financial trauma and catastrophic mistakes. In my own personal experience, talking therapy has helped me to show myself some much-needed compassion, and to identify misplaced guilt that I've been carrying. When you consider that these are both incredibly high hurdles in others' relationships with money, the concept of financial therapy starts to make real sense.

I spoke to Jo Love, mental health ambassador and author of *Therapy is Magic*,[8] about the benefits of therapy for people struggling to make peace with their finances:

CS: Although still sometimes stigmatized, it feels like we're getting to a place where therapy is more normalized for certain life struggles – but I'm not sure that it occurs to many people to seek a therapist when struggling in their relationship with money. Why do you think that is? And what can we do to change it?

JL: It is true, people are starting to talk much more about accessing therapy and slowly that stigma is starting to ease, however there is still a lot of misunderstanding about who can access therapy and what you can go to therapy for. Many people still believe they would not 'qualify' for therapeutic help and there is a common misconception therapy is purely for helping with mental illness recovery rather than maintaining or improving your mental wellness.

In part, this is because much of what is actually discussed inside the therapists' office still remains a secret. You might feel comfortable telling someone you're in therapy but not exactly what you and your therapist talk about. But here's the secret: there is no hierarchy of woe, in which some conditions of life are inherently more misery-making than others. Life is relative – what might be a serious problem for you may be easy for me to cope with, or vice versa. Which means it's about anything and everything you want to discuss, whether that's your mental illness, your childhood, your bank balance, your sex life, your overbearing boss, your annoying neighbour, your interfering mother-in-law: it's all allowed in the therapy room, however big or small. If it matters to you, it matters to your therapist.

Money and our relationship with it are touchy and emotional subjects for many. The more we can do to break down the shame and embarrassment many feel talking about money in general, the more it will help everyone be more honest and open about money and more likely to reach out and get help for any difficulties they might be experiencing, whether that is through therapy, financial advice or other financial support.

CS: In what ways do you think therapy could be helpful for people stuck in a battle with their finances?

JL: The way we treat money is often less linked to logic and reason and more often to unconscious deep-seated emotional beliefs and behaviours we are barely aware of. Therefore, without the right help and guidance it can be near on impossible to break free from any unhealthy patterns, attitudes or relationship with money we might unknowingly have found ourselves in.

Therapy can definitely help to identify and unpick some of the less helpful emotional responses we can have to money and break the cycles that many of us have. And while the thought of talking to a stranger about money might feel exposing, personally, after I've gotten over the initial cringe factor, I've actually found it enormously liberating, not to mention really helpful.

CS: There can be an attitude, especially when money is limited, that therapy is an unaffordable luxury. How do we change that narrative?

JL: While it might seem counter-intuitive to spend money on therapy for financial issues, in the long term it can help with keeping both your mental and financial wellbeing in check and as such, is viewed by many as a necessity rather than a luxury.

Pursuing therapy for whatever reason is a sign of strength, not weakness. We all need help from time to time; if I have a bad tooth, I go to the dentist; if my car breaks down, I go to the mechanic. We get professional support for all kinds of problems, and our mental wellness should be no different.

There are also many free or low-cost options out there, if paying for therapy privately is prohibitive.

Affordable options for therapy and counselling

Given that therapy is a possible gateway towards understanding and accepting your mistakes, or at least getting them off your chest, and allows you a safe space to practise self-forgiveness, in an ideal world I would prescribe it for anyone looking to change their relationship with money. But therapy, and especially good therapy, isn't usually cheap, and chances are that if money is tight, talking therapy is not at the top of your priority list. The ability to discuss and understand your problems with someone who is trained to counsel you through them is framed as a luxury, and so much of the narrative around good money management is that, in times of hardship, the luxuries should be the first things to go. It's hard to prioritize your own needs at the best of times, but if you're dealing with feelings of shame, or of having let yourself or others down because of money issues, it's not likely that you're feeling particularly kind towards yourself, or especially inclined to invest in your own wellbeing. The fact that this is, arguably, the most important time to do it, feels like a cruel irony – as so much about the way that money functions in our society does.

The provision for talking therapy on the NHS is subject to much attention, and the privilege discourse around having a therapist is not going away any time soon. I wrote about this for *Grazia* in early 2021,[9] and when I asked for opinions and experiences, there were an overwhelming number of people wanting to discuss their ordeals – the impossible decisions, the year-long waiting lists, the debt they took on in order to save their mental health.

According to Jo Love, though, there are some avenues for free or affordable therapy that aren't always obvious. Here's her list of avenues that you could explore, if you feel that talking to someone about your relationship with money, and any underlying issues that you might have unearthed, might be good for you, but you feel that cost is a barrier:

1. NHS (speak to your GP, or you can self-refer in most areas online by googling your local Improving Access to Psychological Therapies, or IAPT team).

2. Charities (some offer free counselling and/or telephone listening services). Go have a google!

3. If you are a student, most universities and colleges have free counselling services.

4. Through medical insurance (your own or sometimes you can also access therapy through your partner's, depending on the policy).

5. Through a workplace Employee Assistance Programme. Often you won't even need to say a word to your manager or HR.

6. Online services/apps (please ensure the therapists are registered with a professional body).

7. Ask if a private therapist offers a sliding fee scale or takes on any pro bono cases.

8. Try group therapy, as this is often at a lower cost.

9. Space out your private sessions to give yourself time to save up, or consider batching in 6-week chunks if you prefer the weekly check-in.

Concluding thoughts for Step One

One of the huge material benefits of making peace with your mistakes, and unpacking your financial baggage, is that when you are no longer distracted, or even paralyzed, by feelings of self-blame and shame, it becomes much easier to take positive action towards developing a better relationship with money. For some, smaller or comparatively historical mistakes, you might make the decision that there is nothing that you can or need to do to set things right – and that's absolutely fine. Finding a sense of peace with them, in this case, is enough; case closed.

For bigger or more recent mistakes – those that are still having a material impact on your daily life – you can now start to take the right action to resolve and heal things. When you take shame and self-judgement out of the equation, what you need to do suddenly becomes much clearer, and accessing the right information stops being something to fear, because you're not caught up in the shoulda woulda coulda of things. Taking the sting out of engaging with practical advice was a huge part of finding financial wellbeing for me, and lots of other people that I know. Sometimes, before you can feel informed and empowered, you need to feel supported and understood.

We'll talk about creating practical money rituals in Step Three, and tackling emotional spending in Step Four, but for now it's a good idea to start thinking about what you'd like to change about your relationship with money in practice – the habits that you want to form and the hurdles you'd like to overcome. This could be dealing with legacy debt, refilling your savings after depleting them, starting to build a safety net for the first time – whatever applies to you and your journey. Write yourself a little list, and I'll meet you in Step Two.

Actions for Step One

For each of these five steps, there is a set of actions that you might like to complete in order to really get the most out of this journey and compound some of the theory that we've discussed. To make things extra satisfying, they are formatted as a checklist, so you can tick them off as you go.

- ❏ Put your financial mistakes into context – journal this out, if necessary.
- ❏ Make a list of the internal and external factors that influence or have influenced your relationship with money.
- ❏ Practice meditation for self-trust, and begin to have confidence in your ability to make good decisions.
- ❏ Identify any financial pain or trauma from your past, and look at how it affects your current behaviour.
- ❏ Find somebody to talk to – this could be a trusted friend, family member, partner or professional.

Step Two

Separating your self-worth from your net worth

Over the course of our lives, there are various points where the world reduces us to a series of values on a screen – where someone will look at numbers correlating to decisions that we've made, both good and bad, and make an evaluation. This is, unfortunately, they way that lots of our financial systems operate – applying for car finance or a mortgage, or even to rent a home – and it causes anxiety and shame and a whole host of other unpleasant feelings. **But it does not mean that you have to do the same thing to yourself.** You know that you are more than a list of numbers on a screen or a spreadsheet. You are not your credit score or your consumer debt, you are not your savings or your investments or your pension. All of these things have the power to impact your life – to make things easier or harder, to make you feel more stressed or more relaxed – but they have absolutely nothing to do with who you are. None of these values should have the power to dictate your self-worth, and yet for so many of us, they do.

I've spoken to lots of different people over the course of my career about the relationship between how they feel about money and how they feel about themselves. People in all kinds of financial situations, from all kinds of different backgrounds, each of them with a different history of struggling in some way with their relationship with money. And for each and every one of them, their relationship with money is completely inextricable from their relationship with themselves. It's inextricable from what they think of themselves, from the esteem that they hold themselves in. Some people cling desperately to every penny they earn, believing that they are only worth what they can save. Some people spend everything in sight, and then some, because they don't believe they're worthy of financial peace. Some climb the career ladder furiously, in search of a salary that will make them feel that they've finally arrived, while others are afraid to negotiate better pay because they don't believe that they're worth it. There are so many ways in which your relationship with money can be broken – but that doesn't mean that it can't be fixed.

Deriving your self-worth from your net worth might mean that:

- You struggle to see a way out of financial difficulty.
- You don't feel deserving of the money that you have or the salary that you earn.
- You constantly strive for more and more money, and it never feels like enough.

- You feel locked in cycles of damaging financial behaviour.
- You struggle to let go of money or to spend on anything but the essentials.
- You overspend habitually but never get any satisfaction from your purchases.
- You put undue importance on status symbols or wealth signifiers.

Money and self-worth are so closely linked for most people that we sometimes struggle to see the wood for the trees, like two necklaces so completely tangled that you can no longer tell what strand belongs to which chain. Extricating them can be a lengthy and frustrating process, but sometimes, if you pull on the right knot, everything loosens, and it gets easier to untangle the rest. The more that you can understand about the relationship between your self-worth and your finances, the easier it becomes to pull them apart, and to appreciate your worth beyond its measurement in dollars or euro or pounds sterling. In this step, we'll explore the many ways in which they are linked, in order to help you to find that weak spot to attack and unravel. This isn't an instant fix – it might take time for you to start feeling the effects of the insights you uncover and the changes that you make, but it's so important for a healthy relationship with your money and yourself.

Having a difficult relationship with money does not mean that you are:

- Lazy or workshy
- Irresponsible or untrustworthy
- 'Silly' or unintelligent
- Greedy or superficial

It might mean that you:

- Have unresolved issues from the past
- Haven't taken the time to assess your priorities
- Were never taught how to manage money
- Have made some poor decisions

There's no such thing as 'bad with money'

When I started engaging with the world of personal finance, especially on social media, I was drawn into the world of money bloggers and self-proclaimed personal finance experts. This space is absolutely choc-full of useful information, often portrayed in ways that are easier to access and digest than more traditional media. In fact, part of the reason that these communities have grown and thrived so much is that the world of traditional finance is (rightly, in my opinion) perceived as stuffy and inaccessible, built for people who already have a lot of money and just need to decide what to do with it. Certainly, that's the way that I had always felt about those spheres – shut out and inadequate. Now, though, there is a wealth of different ways to access financial information, and mainstream organizations are having to work hard to try and bring their communication strategy into the twenty-first century, a good twenty years too late.

So, these communities, on Facebook, Instagram and even TikTok, have grown into platforms for education and connection, which is an undoubtedly good thing. But the shame and judgement are still there. There are endless TikToks, Reels and carousel posts dictating exactly what it means to be 'good with money', what constitutes 'good debt' and 'bad debt', which leads me to wonder: when is the moralizing of money going to end? Who is one person to decide what it means to be 'good with money'? It's completely subjective, surely.

All that is achieved by narratives such as this is that people in need of guidance feel ashamed and alienated, and are therefore prevented from accessing the information that they need. It undermines people's confidence, creating and perpetuating self-fulfilling prophecies about being 'bad with money'. It creates a feeling of panic, followed by a knee-jerk reaction – which is, in my experience, very rarely the starting point for lasting and sustainable change. In reality, being 'good with money' means different things to different people – there's no one-size-fits-all prescription. Not everybody needs to live by the same plan, because not everyone has the same goals in sight or resources at their disposal. No matter how much we're encouraged to participate in the rat race, we really don't need to compare and compete with people whose origins and aspirations are wildly different from our own.

This isn't to say that it doesn't matter at all how you manage your money, only that you shouldn't be measuring your own financial success by the yardstick of a stranger on the internet. So, if we're not aiming for 'good with money', what are we aiming for?

That's right: financial wellbeing. We need to stop looking at external measures of how 'good' or 'bad' we are with money, and gauge our financial health by how successfully we're looking after our own financial wellbeing.

Changing how we measure our worth

We are all so much more than the sum of our parts. We exist, and our existence is valid and valuable no matter how good our relationship with money is. We know this, and yet we still look for external validation – for facts and figures and opinions that tell us we're doing okay, that we're worth something. That we're a good person. That we're well liked. That we're competent, clever, kind. I talk a lot throughout this book about the internal and external factors that influence our relationship with money, and the focus of this chapter is on learning how we can tame them both. How we can look at those external factors – our bank balance, feedback at work, guidance from professionals – and hold on to it only for as long as it is useful. To take the information that we need without letting it permeate too deeply, without letting it stagnate as shame or fear. This is not something that I've been very good at in the past. Accepting criticism or bad outcomes without beating myself up is something that I've always found very difficult, and sometimes it's kept me locked in a cycle of not really trying hard enough and then being disappointed by the results. Because what if you give it your all and it's still not good enough? That's terrifying to me.

And yet we have to find a way to overcome that fear if we want to thrive, because when we tie our worth to external values and then panic about measuring up, all we do is limit our potential – and this applies just as much to money as it does to anything else. When we see certain cash values and figures as being associated with our intrinsic worth as a person, it can lead to an unhealthy obsession with accumulating wealth in order to try to increase our perceived value, or, alternatively, we can become stuck in a mindset of not pushing for what we deserve because we believe that our value is set at a certain point.

So, if not with a monetary value, how do we measure our worth? Well, my first question here is why do we feel the need to measure it at all? In fact, how could we possibly do it? As far as I'm aware, there's no unit of measurement that could possibly be adequate, so instead we have to find another way to think about things. Our value – whether as a friend, colleague, employee, contractor, romantic partner or family member – is constantly in flux. There are things that we can do and change to be of more value to others, whether for altruistic reasons, such as giving our time or energy to someone we care about, or out of self-interest, such as increasing your value to your company or manager so that you can feel secure in your role, progress or confidently ask for a pay rise. But your worth is constant. Your worth does not depend on what you can offer to other people, how much money is in your bank account or how successfully you manage your finances. Remembering that will give you something to push off from every time you need to stand up for yourself or make difficult decisions. It will carry you through difficult times, through letting people down or disappointing yourself, and stop you from getting dragged under. It will protect you from feeling as if you need to chase whichever opportunity will give you more money and status throughout your life, and allow you to prioritize happiness and wellbeing.

It matters how we make our money, as well as how we spend it

So much of the discussion around money and self-worth focusses on how we spend it, which is certainly very important, but there is also something to be said about how we make our money, and how that relates to our feelings of self-worth. Our complex relationship with money often extends to include our relationship with work – how much we value the work that we do, the societal perception of our job, how good we think we are at it. The generation before mine in my family – my parents, my aunts and uncles – are or were all public servants in some way, shape or form. Teachers, nurses, social workers; all contributing something to society, those noble roles that newspapers and politicians are keen to slap a 'hero' sticker on without ever supporting fair pay or working conditions.

This interplay between our money and our work is present for everybody, but I've found it to be particularly fraught for freelance and self-employed people. Anna Codrea-Rado, journalist, activist and author of freelancer guide *You're the Business*, agrees.[1]

'When you're employed by someone else, you're paid for your input. You put in the work, and you take your salary home at the end of each month, regardless. But when you work for yourself, you get paid for your output – and if something affects your ability to deliver the work, your finances are directly affected,' she says. This is something that I had to grapple with fairly early on in my own journey with money. Not long after I started writing about my debt, and my relationship with money, I had to leave my job at a start-up to save my rapidly declining mental health, launching a free-lance career with absolutely no safety net and a five-figure sum of debt to service. It was a huge risk, and not something that I could, in good conscience, recommend to anyone else. It paid off eventually, though in the short-term it did com-plicate things somewhat. I noticed the changes in my relation-ship with money almost immediately, in ways both good and bad. Having to pay close attention to every single thing that came in and went out of my account, and having to have conversations about rates and fees, helped me to engage with my finances and to feel less awkward talking about money. I started to realize that there wasn't really a cap on my earnings as there had been when I was employed – something which, most self-employed people will agree, can be both a blessing and a curse.

For all the benefits of earning and engaging with money in a new way, and for all the relief I felt as I moved away from the frustrations of trying to progress in my career according to somebody else's terms, there were new challenges. For the first time ever, *I* was the one deciding what my work was worth, and setting my rates was something I struggled with for a long time – as lots of freelancers do. Even though I was earning more per unit of my time, I felt that my self-worth was even more tied to my earnings than ever before, and I struggled to say no to work or safeguard any of my personal time. I started to see my minutes and hours for their cash value, and any moment that I wasn't working was a missed opportunity to pay a little more off my debt, or to put a little extra into an emergency fund. I also experienced the typical freelancer anxiety around turning down any opportunity, in case it was the last one.

Then, there was the fear of 'selling out'. I was finally – after years of earning a salary in marketing and feeling increasingly guilty about contributing to a problem that I myself was struggling with – doing work that I was proud of. I was being vulnerable, finally able to be truly myself in my work, and helping others in the course of doing so – but I had to be able to find a way to make a living too. This felt particularly sensitive because of the subject matter of my work, and sure enough, the first accusations of being a sell-out materialized on the Instagram post where I announced the impending publication of my first book, *Real Life Money*. I grappled with my conscience every time I posted about my book, worrying that people would think I was a hypocrite, or that I was just trying to make money from the vulnerable people in my audience. At the same time, when I started writing for publications and negotiating brand and advertising partnerships, I worried that this too constituted selling out. Some deals were far more lucrative than any work I'd ever done before, and I would squeamishly compare the rates with the days and weeks I would have had to work to earn that much in my old job. I worried about getting an overblown sense of my own value, and what the consequences of that might be. The whole thing really made me confront and consider a lot of the assumptions and beliefs that I had about money, and the way that I moralized earning what I considered to be a fortune.

As time has moved on, I've become more comfortable with this new way of working and earning, and I've worked hard to separate my sense of self-worth from the money that I earn. One of the things that has helped is the fact that my husband works in a very different, employed role. Until very recently, he had always earned quite a lot more than me, especially during the years when I was working part time to accommodate our young children. Different couples take different approaches to how they manage money in their relationships, but we have always shared money, through the really awful times, and now in overwhelmingly better ones. Seeing the different ways that we work and earn, the way that they complement one another and the different value that they hold has helped me to reach a more peaceful place with regard to how I earn a living. I earn more, but he has the steady salary, so when it comes to saving to buy a house, as we're currently doing, I'm able to put more cash aside for the deposit, but his very decent, steady salary is the golden key to a mortgage. So, my suggestion to you, if you are experiencing any sense of anxiety around earning 'too much' as a freelancer, particularly in comparison to a previous salary, is to converse more and compare less. Speak to the people in your life about their ways of working and earning, read articles and maybe even Twitter. Talk to enough people and you will soon see that there are hundreds upon thousands of different ways of working and earning and, more importantly, that you earning more does not directly relate to somebody else earning less or vice versa. Consider the value of your work, the way that it makes you feel, and the future that it is helping you to build. Remember that money is not a scarce resource in the world, rather that it is unfairly distributed in absolute extremes. It is, of course, entirely possible to be self-employed and barely getting by, with many factors such as health, childcare, resources and working capital limiting your ability to earn more. There is no 'right' way to work and earn as a self-employed person, which can be both freeing and terrifying. Rather than having parameters drawn for us by an employer, we have to draw our own – and sometimes that includes saying no to more money in exchange for more time or liveable working conditions. It's a tightrope act – and one where the rope keeps changing thickness at that.

I've managed, largely, to reach sense of peace with the notion of having in some way 'sold out'. For most of us, there is a feeling of conflict between our desire for change to a system that oppresses people, perpetuates poverty cycles and destroys the planet in the way that late capitalism undeniably does, and our wish to survive – even thrive – within that same system. The phrase 'money is the root of all evil' – which relates to this same system – is something that many of us have coded into our DNA, and it can make us feel anxious or ashamed about wanting more of it, even if the lifestyle that we're striving for is relatively modest. It's something that I also grapple with, but we all have to find a balance that fits with our own values, beliefs and aspirations, and I know that I'm doing that to the best of my ability. And it's none of my business whether someone else thinks I've sold out. But all of these different conflicts about the way that we work can play into our relationship with money, and distort its value and virtue in our minds, and we feel that more acutely,

I believe, when our earnings are tied directly to our output or performance.

Similarly, being underpaid in a role that we love, or give a lot of our time and energy to, or both, can start to seep into our sense of what we feel we're worth. Working yourself into the ground while simultaneously struggling to keep up with your outgoings is cruelly common in our stretched society, and especially in the public sector, where pay is dictated by central government as opposed to being related to performance or decided by your boss. A lack of pay mobility can make people feel undervalued and stuck. Let's not underestimate the toll that those feelings can have on your relationship with money either. When I was working sixty-hour weeks for a £16k salary after graduating from university, I developed an incredibly cavalier attitude towards my spending habits, and it landed me in a payday loan-shaped hole of trouble. I saw my hard work as a currency in itself, and I spent according to what I felt I deserved, rather than what I was actually earning. It's difficult, without a career change that often comes with its own financial impossibilities, to see how this can be overcome. The social-preneur (i.e those whose success is either driven by or displayed proudly on social media) discourse that we're used to seeing, particularly in some circles, can be scathing about the choice to stay in the 9–5 'trap', but a lot of people *like* their jobs and feel that they're making a difference, as well as benefitting from the security that employment lends you – they just want to be paid fairly for their time. What's important here, as well as exploring avenues to increase your income if it truly is keeping you trapped in a lifestyle that's not making you happy, is to actually acknowledge the way that you're feeling. Being undervalued by your employer, whether in the private sector or the public sector (which, according to teacher friends of mine, actually feels a lot like being undervalued by society itself) is not something that remains at the office. You carry it with you into your home, into your sense of wellbeing and into your habits with money.

• • •

I'd like you to start thinking about your relationship with work and earning, and how it feeds into your wider relationship with money. Do you earn a salary, are you self-employed, or both? Do you see money earned as a side-hustle or passion project in a different light to how you see a salaried income? Has your income changed over the last few years, and has your attitude towards the money that you're earning shifted in line with that? Sometimes, as we start to progress in our careers and make more money, we start to feel a sense of guilt or of being undeserving – does that resonate with you? Or perhaps you've spent years feeling underpaid and overworked – is this something that affects how you feel about money? In order to achieve a full sense of financial wellbeing, these are things that we need to unpack and work through. Again, I recommend getting something down on paper here; writing can be magical, in that sometimes our true feelings seem to bypass our conscious thoughts and end up on the paper almost by themselves, which can really help with your understanding of the relationship between how you work, how you earn, and how you feel about money.

Your worth is not defined by:

- How much money you have in the bank
- The balance on your credit card
- The number on the scales
- How much you earn
- How many times a week you exercise
- How many emails you sent today
- Any other number

Is constantly striving for more doing us more harm than good?

'Since these conveniences by becoming habitual had almost entirely ceased to be enjoyable, and at the same time degenerated into true needs, it became much more cruel to be deprived of them than to possess them was sweet, and men were unhappy to lose them without being happy to possess them.'

Jean-Jacques Rousseau

Even within a system that is constantly pelting us with non-verbal cues that we need to know our place and be happy with our lot, modern culture is determinedly pushing us not to settle for less than we are worth. The rise of 'girlboss culture' throughout the 2010s encouraged women to challenge the system, and to be loud about it, in the name of feminism, and though there has been something of a reckoning for this movement (which mainly centred around wealthy white women and still seemed to measure a person's value by the same patriarchal, capitalist yardstick as before), there are still some relics of it in the way that we view success in the 2020s. As we watched female-only club The Wing and other artefacts of selective feminism dissolve into a pile of scalloped pink tiles and mustard velvet following allegations of racism, ablism and bullying,[2] we were forced to confront our own ideas about true success vs the perception of success. There has to be a balance that we can strike between languishing in a state of despondency and discontent and pushing ourselves so hard towards an arbitrary, moving idea of success that we burn out before we even get to enjoy the fruits of our labour. It's the same with money, and, in fact, given how closely work and money are related, our career and financial goals should usually align if we're hoping to encourage financial wellbeing.

This is where the hedonic treadmill theory is useful to us in explaining why nothing we ever do – no promotion, no amount of money, no level of material comfort – ever feels enough. Why our achievements, whether in our financial, personal or work lives, quickly fade into insignificance once we actually achieve them. The hedonic treadmill, or hedonic adaption, can be used to explain so much of what goes wrong in our relationship with money and the way that it affects our self-worth. It posits that we all have a baseline level of happiness, and any move away from that baseline – either negative or positive – will be temporary.[3] This set point of wellbeing means that, as much as we have coveted and strived for a certain job, a certain salary, a certain amount of money in the bank, we will eventually get used to it, and the joy that we feel at having achieved it fades. We immediately move the goalposts, and our baseline for contentment moves in line with them. Our achievements are never enough for us, because we default to the same level of happiness after a while. This tends to be compounded by other things, such as our tendency to 'upgrade' our lifestyle as our means increase, and the fact that our social circles may change as our income and stage of our career does. In his *A Theory of Human Motivation*,[4] Abraham H. Maslow suggests that 'man is a perpetually wanting animal' – i.e. as we fulfil the needs in our hierarchy, we move on to create new needs to fulfil.

Understanding this is important for financial wellbeing because it helps us to realize that even if we put an empirical value on our self-worth, there's no guarantee that when we reach it, we'll finally feel content. In fact, all of the evidence suggests that we won't. Our brains just keep moving the target, and we keep pushing on. The treadmill keeps going until we are completely burnt out and ready to drop.

So, I'm guessing that what you'd like to know now is whether there's anything we can do to stop this constant adaption, whether there is a big red stop button that we can press when our legs start to get wobbly. The good news is that there is – the bad news is that it's hard. If you're relying on external forces to let you know that you've finally made it, you will stay on that treadmill forever. Nobody is going to put a hand on your shoulder and tell you that you've done enough, that you have enough – you have to come to that realization for yourself.

It's not likely that any salary, or any amount of money in the bank, in savings or investments, is ever going to feel like enough – and not because you're greedy or insatiable, but because of the effects of hedonic adaption and the fact that you exist in a system where you will never run out of things to buy or ways to upgrade your lifestyle and comfort in accordance with your means. So, you have to start setting your own framework for fulfilment, and also accepting that sometimes achieving a goal doesn't feel like a lightning bolt of ecstasy, but something gentler and more subtle. Accept that you won't be able to alter that happiness set point in any meaningful way by getting more and more stuff, or seeing those numbers in your account inflate, and start looking at other ways to increase your happiness in smaller, everyday increments.

• • •

Gratitude practice has made its way into the mainstream over the last decade or so, with most people working in the wellbeing space agreeing that it plays a huge role in fostering feelings of happiness and fulfilment. Regular active gratitude can help you to move that set point of happiness over time, because it helps you to pull what you have into sharp focus, rather than putting all of the emphasis on what you don't have. It's easy to see how this could also benefit your financial wellbeing at the same time as making you feel generally happier – it's one of the places where the link is strongest. Many different courses and plans to improve wellbeing include daily gratitudes – focussing on just two or three things that you are grateful for, which you either write down or actively think about – and I believe this has a key role in your journey towards financial health. It helps to strengthen the muscles that you need to fight off the constant torrent of FOMO marketing, and reduces the need to keep levelling up. We'll talk about gratitude practice and how to develop rituals and habits around it a little more in Step Three.

As with gratitude, many of the recommended techniques for beating hedonic adaption are repeated actions rather than single events, which they also have in common with some of the habits and rituals that we'll talk about later. A couple of things to try to incorporate into your daily life now, in the hope of shifting that happiness set point even just a few degrees in the right direction and reducing that feeling of needing to constantly level up your earning, spending and lifestyle choices, are:

Delayed gratification

This means trying to keep short-term bursts of satisfaction in perspective, and sometimes choosing to forego them in order to achieve a bigger, longer-lasting sense of happiness later on. In the context of money, this might mean avoiding spending on frivolous things, or things that you don't see any long-term value in, in favour of experiencing a better sense of financial security long-term.

As we'll discuss later, our brains are biased towards the decision that will give us the most instant hit of satisfaction, even if there is a far greater win to be had in the future. Our brains prefer instant gratification, which is why it's so tempting to skip an exercise session in favour of Netflix even though we know we'll feel stronger and calmer later if we hit the gym. It's also why we might struggle to control the urge to snack when we know we have a lovely meal ahead of us shortly, or to make impulse purchases when what we really want is to save for a house deposit. The further away the gratification is, the more tempting the stopgap becomes, even when it's actively detrimental to our big goal.

In practising delayed gratification, we allow ourselves to enjoy the process of getting somewhere. We take the focus off the little, short-lived pings of pleasure and energy that we get from those instant gratifications, and start to enjoy steady progress and the journey as a whole.

Flow/being present in the moment

Being fully immersed or involved in an activity can really increase your happiness, because it allows you to let go of some of the general life baggage that we all carry around with us – the worries and fears, the guilt and shame that are all part of being an adult human. Doing this repeatedly, whatever the activity (think gardening, dance, yoga, running, reading etc) can have a similar effect to meditation, in that it gives us a bit of a break from our internal monologue, and this in turn can improve our happiness.

You're probably familiar with mindfulness, which we'll discuss in greater detail later on, and mindful behaviours can be a great antidote to the hedonic pressures of modern life. Flow, or allowing yourself to be fully present in the moment, is one of the core elements of mindfulness, and the wonderful thing about it is that you can apply it to whatever interests you. You might like to revisit a hobby that you loved during your childhood, or you might listen to music that you love, really loudly, until it fills your whole body and leaves no room for niggling feelings of not being enough. You could immerse yourself in stories or conversations, or learn a new language – anything that gives you a break from your own thoughts for a little while, on a regular basis.

Pleasure

This is more about those fleeting moments of joy and satisfaction that we usually associate with the word 'happy', and finding more ways to build these small moments into our everyday lives. They give us something to look forward to, and can have a halo effect on everything else, colouring even the mundane but necessary moments of life with their glow. Take something that gives you that little moment of release and think about where you might be able to duplicate that feeling throughout your day or week. It might be the first sip that you take of your coffee in the morning, or the rush of wind in your hair when you cycle down a hill, or a proper belly laugh at a favourite TV show.

If you're concerned about finding time for these moments, can you use them to replace the times when you do things mindlessly? Can you catch yourself when you're 'doom scrolling' Twitter, and tell yourself 'enough'? Saying, 'That's enough, I'm going to do something that gives me pleasure now' shouldn't be a radical act, but it often feels like it is. We can shy away from pleasure, especially if we feel undeserving of it, but it's so, so important. The more pleasure we are able to squeeze out of the little moments of our lives, the less we need to tell ourselves that we'll be happy when we finally get that dress, those shoes, that car, that house.

• • •

Fostering a sense of contentment and fulfilment, and kicking against the instinct to spend our whole lives striving for more is important for our general wellbeing and happiness, but it's also a really sound financial habit too. When we don't put too much pressure on our financial status to fill a hole, and when we find ways to improve our quality of life without relying on accruing more and more material possessions, we might find that habits like overspending, saving obsessively, overworking ourselves or ignoring our finances start to naturally dissipate. We'll discuss our emotional relationship with spending in more detail a little later on, but for now, I'd really like you to think about some times in your life when you've felt content. They could be fleeting or sustained, joyous or simply calm. Now, I'd like you to think about your money habits around that time. Were they calmer and more relaxed? Did you feel less of a compulsion to spend?

Interestingly, much of our culture tells us that, in the relationship between success (and the material benefits of that success, such as money) and happiness, the causation is weighted towards success – i.e. success makes you happy, but psychologists have also argued convincingly that the opposite is true, and that the flow can happen in the other direction.[5] Being happy can make you successful too – but you have to get off the treadmill.

I'd now like you to start thinking about these methods for combatting hedonic adaption, and how you might be able to apply them to your own life. Be really honest with yourself about what it is that you're striving for, and whether or not you expect achieving a particular financial goal to solve other problems. Are you relying on hitting your house deposit total to start feeling less anxious about money? Do you think that becoming debt-free will dissolve all of your money shame along with it too? Because, if so, you might find yourself disappointed when you do get there. After the initial jubilation, you might find yourself looking around, wondering what has really changed – you might feel empty or unsatisfied, and that is the very last thing you should be feeling when you hit these amazing achievements.

Ways to get off the hedonic treadmill:

- Focus on the pleasurable moments in your life – make a list and aim to fill as much of your time as possible with them.
- Find something that you love to do, that quietens the voices telling you that you aren't enough.
- Be patient. Not everything is meant to come to you right away.
- Take pleasure in the journey towards a goal, and stop putting all of the pressure on the moment that you arrive there.

The green-eyed monster

One of the things that can seriously detract from our baseline happiness and make it more difficult for us to jump off the hedonic treadmill is envy. Envy is part of being human, but God knows it's not the nicest feeling in the world. I do often think that envy gets a bad rap, considering it's something that we all feel, at least from time to time – and something that we have absolutely no control over at that. It's seen as an ugly trait, something to be ashamed of, especially if what we're coveting is money.

Envy can actually be useful in some ways, because it can help us to figure out what we want. For most of us, envy isn't about not wanting to see other people being successful, rather that we want some of that success for ourselves – and there is plenty of success to go around. I've had to work through a lot of money-related envy in my life, particularly in the second half of my twenties, when I was struggling to balance the books and cover childcare while my close childhood friends bought houses and went on far-flung holidays. It wasn't that I didn't want those things for them – of course I did – but I wanted them too. The main thing that I was envious of, though, was the peace of mind that seemed to come with being free to make positive decisions with money. All of my own decisions at the time were based on what would be the least bad outcome – I was fighting fires rather than building anything. I was envious of the fact that they didn't have the burden of their poor decisions weighing down on them, as I did. It wasn't a very nice feeling, and it added to the guilt that I already felt about the financial difficulty my family was in – how awful must I be as a person, if I couldn't even feel properly happy for my friends?

It's important to remember that feeling envious every now and again is completely normal, and as long as the green-eyed monster is a transient beast and doesn't linger for too long, it's unlikely that there will be any lasting effect on your relationships or sense of self-worth. But if envy and resentment are left to linger, or allowed to remain unchallenged, they can leave a serious dent in your happiness and hamper your ability to appreciate any of the good things in your own life. What's more, when we consider hedonic adaption, it becomes clear that even if we were to gain the thing that we've been coveting – the thing that *that* person has, that we don't – it would be unlikely to have a lasting effect on our happiness anyway. This applies to any type of envy – professional, personal, or financial.

I'd like to give you the opportunity here to work through any feelings of envy that you're harbouring at the moment. Consider who they are directed at, how strong they are and how long you've been holding on to them. Now, ask yourself how you would feel if you gained that coveted thing, whether it's a job, a possession, a certain amount of money. Have you been pinning all of your imaginings of happiness and fulfilment on this one thing? Do you think that's a realistic view of things? Think about how that jealousy is affecting your happiness at the moment – is it stopping you from being able to appreciate what you actually have? Is it holding you back from taking steps towards a similar goal of your own? Is it making you spend more than you can afford, because you think that you deserve those things too?

With feelings that are as uncomfortable and stigmatized as envy, you might have to tease them out bit by bit. This exercise requires fairly radical honesty with yourself, and that's not always the most pleasant experience, but it will really help you to understand some of the ways in which you might be acting as a barrier to your own sense of wellbeing.

Exercise: Understanding your financial envy

For this exercise, I'd like you to try to put aside any judgement of yourself or of others. First, I'd like you to make a list of all of the things that make you envious with regards to money. They could be close to home, such as a friend managing to buy a house ahead of you, or as far-flung as the houses you've seen on *Selling Sunset*. Next, really interrogate where that envy comes from. Why do you want those things – is it really the money or material wealth that you're envious of, or is it the luxury of time, or the peace of mind that can come with having more disposable cash? Then, if you like, you can start to think about ways that you can foster those feelings in your own life – but often just looking at our envy directly rather than shrinking away from it can loosen its hold on us and diminish its influence on our mindset and behaviour.

People-pleasing is a financial burden

When I started to discover where I'd gone wrong in my relationship with money, it didn't take long for one factor to come to the fore – something that had influenced my decisions again and again, from the kitchen of my hostel house-share in Australia to the newsfeed of my personal Instagram account. Other people. The weight of their opinions, the desire to impress them, the desperation not to disappoint them. My own sense of self was always in second place, and not even a close second, to the perception of me that other people had. I had a very clear idea of how I wanted to be seen, the impression that I wanted other people to have of me, and the financial cost of achieving that was not something I ever really considered.

For a very long time, praise from others was my nectar, the only thing sustaining me, keeping me from spinning off into an in-depth study of all of the things that were wrong with me. I came alive when I was making other people happy, but on my own I felt insufficient and unappealing. I let the lines blur between myself and those whose approval I sought, and I lived that way from my early teens until my late twenties. I had no idea how to have a relationship that didn't rely on transactions where I always had to be the one to give more. As I started to work on my financial situation, started to notice how connected some of my worst and most nonsensical decisions were to my almost non-existent self-esteem, I was suddenly faced with the sheer number of different ways in which trying to please or impress other people can cost you financially. There are the obvious, direct things, such as gift-giving and being unable to say no to expensive plans with other people, and then there are the wider ripple effects, such as spending on yourself as a pick-me-up because you're too busy looking after others to meet your own basic needs. Since I was quite young, I've been an obsessive gift-giver. Only the perfect gift will do – thoughtful, expensive, meticulously chosen. If there's an inside joke, throwback or deeper spiritual meaning, even better.

The problem with putting all of your resources into other people is that the feeling of having satisfied someone else's needs doesn't last long. It needs to be constantly topped up, and we end up ignoring our own needs in favour of becoming a sort of buffet of emotional resources for those around us – a constant conveyor belt of little portions of our energy, doled out to others before we ever take any for ourselves. We don't put our own oxygen masks on before assisting others and, after a while, this 'selflessness' – which actually stems from a desire to be liked – becomes expected by others, and it's even harder for us to change our behaviour without fearing that we will offend or hurt them.

One of the most common pieces of advice I'm asked to give is how to say no to other people where money is concerned –

either people who are asking to borrow it or, more often, when those close to you have a bigger budget and higher expectations for things like nights out, weddings and group trips. This can be even more intense in romantic partnerships where one person earns more than the other. For a very long time this stumped me, because wanting to please people and be perceived as likeable was my own Achilles heel – how could I advise others to 'just say no' when it was something that I struggled with myself? I wasn't very well-versed in how to set boundaries, which is something that I've spent a lot of time working on over the last year. Around the time when *Real Life Money* was published and I felt my boundaries crumble like a misjudged Bake-Off showstopper, I discovered therapist Nedra Glover Tawwab on Instagram.[6] She is a boundaries expert, and when her first book, *Set Boundaries, Find Peace*,[7] was published in 2021, I was keen to get my hands on it. From the first few pages, it resonated so deeply with me that it felt almost like a violent attack. I realized just how deep-seated my own boundary issues were – even the ones that I'd already begun to work on – and the ripple effect that they were having on so much of my life. I saw clearly how responsible my failure to commit to and communicate healthy boundaries was for the burn-out I was experiencing, and the creeping resentment that I was feeling. I knew that I couldn't hope to protect my growing sense of financial wellbeing without introducing new boundaries and strengthening the ones that I already had in place – that if I didn't do this work then my financial health would always, in some capacity, be dictated by those around me.

I'd like you to think about the extent to which this is true for you. Are you a people-pleaser? Can you think of occasions when not having clear boundaries cost you your financial health? Are there ways in which you've sacrificed your financial stability and peace of mind because you wanted to feel accepted, or because you didn't feel that you could say no to someone else?

This can be one of the issues with our societal reluctance to talk honestly about money. With a lack of accurate information available, we run the risk of making assumptions about what everyone else is working with, which can be damaging to both us and them. After all, the way in which we're all pushed to finance our lifestyles with quick credit means that it's entirely possible to present an affluent or at least comfortable lifestyle on the surface while struggling horribly with money in reality. All of which also means that, without any further insight, people might assume that a hen weekend in Barcelona or even after-work drinks are affordable for you, even when they're not, and can lead to a situation in which you're forced to decide whether to be honest and protect your financial health or to keep up appearances and stick it on a credit card.

Our worth isn't defined by what we buy for other people

On a related note, this issue – how our sense of worth is sometimes linked to our buying power in relation to others – is a big one for me. There is an assumption among a lot of people that emotional spending and living beyond your means is a purely selfish thing. And while I'm sure that this is the case for some, I would like to politely call bullshit, because I think they are a minority. Most people I know tend to spend in response to some kind of pull on their heartstrings.

When I finished paying off my debt and suddenly had a lot more money available to me, my first thought wasn't about what goal I should be focussing on now – it was about who I could buy things for. How I could make up for money being so tight over the previous few years by showing people that I cared in the way that I've been taught to show them – by buying them things.

Generosity is a truly wonderful quality, and one that I think is sometimes undervalued, but there is something flawed in the way that we view generosity in today's society. More often than not, we are encouraged to see generosity – both other people's and our own – in relation to its cash value. This is often exacerbated around gift-giving season, and particularly Christmas, but it exists all year round. I've certainly been guilty in the past of disregarding acts of kindness and generosity that didn't manifest in the form of desirable objects, of being ungrateful for the thought and effort that people I love have put into a gesture. This is something that seems to be actively encouraged by the society and culture that we live in – dependent as our economy is on people continuing to buy things they don't want or need in order to try to make up for time and connection that they have lost.

In December 2020, Currys PC World put out a Christmas TV advert in the UK that centred around the idea of gifting. The whole premise of the storyline was people giving terrible gifts, and having to witness the disappointment of the people they care about – the items in question were things like board games and stuffed animals. The ad then showed those same people giving expensive electronic gifts to their loved ones, with the solution being presented as Currys PC World's 'buy now, pay later', service in order to finance them. Complaints were made to the Advertising Standards Agency (ASA), and were upheld,[8] for reasons that are, to be frank, glaringly obvious to me. The report, and the comments from the advertising agency, make very interesting reading. I'll talk more about manipulative advertising in Step Four, but for now, I want to focus on the pre-existing beliefs that the advertisers were hoping to tap into with this campaign.

Most of us worry all the time about whether we are good enough. Good enough at work, good enough for our friends, our children, our partners. And consumer culture presents us with a quick, easy cure for feeling guilty or inadequate – gifts! We're encouraged to replace time and shared experiences with material demonstrations of our affection, and it never feels like enough. Then, we have to work harder in order to maintain or even increase the level of gifting that we now feel is expected, and we lose out on more time and connection. It never ends.

Exercise: Unpacking our need to spend on other people

Think about the role that this plays in your life. Are there ways that you perpetuate a cycle of feeling inadequate and trying to make up for lost time or to assuage guilt by buying things for other people? Does it now feel impossible to stop that snowball effect? How does it really make you feel? Are you feeling used up? Burnt out? Harassed or resentful? There are a few ways that we can try to resolve those feelings and move forward to healthier ways of expressing love and generosity, but almost all of these things involve figuring out and enforcing new boundaries.

Ways to be generous without overspending:

- Write a thoughtful letter
- Take the time to really listen to someone
- Share skills, resources and insights
- Pass on or share things that you already have
- Offer your time, or a non-financial favour

Boundaries are a sound investment

I mentioned before that boundaries have never been a strong suit of mine, and it's made things really difficult when it comes to protecting my own financial stability and wellbeing.

When we talk about overcoming the need to please other people, boundaries are one of the key resolutions that comes up time and time again. In her book, *Untamed*, Glennon Doyle recalls googling what she should do about her cheating husband, because he was also a great father. She spent hours reading different opinions, but rather than finding it bewildering, she drew empowerment from the conflicting advice. She describes a moment where she realized that, as hard as she tried, she could not do what all of these people thought was best. She could not please everyone, and so she learned to listen to herself.[9]

There will always be people who will think you spend too much on X and not enough on Y. There will always be people who do not understand or agree with how you earn, save, invest and spend your money, and they might not always be strangers on the internet. They might be your close friends and family, people you admire, those with the power to persuade you. So, you have to learn to have the courage of your own convictions, to listen to yourself and trust yourself, all of which we've covered – but these things are impossible to hold on to without properly enforced and upheld boundaries. If you want to focus on your own wellbeing, financial or otherwise, it is necessary to protect your progress and healing from those who would try – intentionally or not – to sabotage it.

I grew up afraid of boundaries, because I didn't want to be cold or closed off. My childhood heroine, the famously unboundaried and free-spirited Anne Shirley from *Anne of Green Gables*, would never put up walls between herself and anyone but Gilbert Blythe – and even that didn't last for ever. I thought that to be boundaried was to be selfish, and the example set by my (wonderful) mother was that you give away as much of yourself as you possibly can in the hope of making others happy. But what I've realized since is that it doesn't work. It leaves you empty and anxious, and the needs of others are still just as vast and insatiable. Money is one of many resources that we need to lead a good life, and I've found that it is almost always acutely affected by any boundary issues that we might have. It's normal to worry about putting new boundaries in place, especially when it comes to money – when your relationships mean a lot to you, it's natural to worry about anything that poses a potential risk to the closeness you have with those you care about. Nobody wants to be perceived as 'tight' or 'mean', even though those labels will inevitably mean different things to different people, and preserving enough of our resources to achieve a sense of happiness and wellbeing for ourselves should never be anything to be ashamed of.

It's worth noting that having healthy boundaries isn't only about what we give away – it's about what we take on. We absorb so many ideas and judgements by osmosis from the headlines and from social media that we can become ashamed and anxious without even really knowing where those feelings are coming from. If we're not careful, we can find ourselves trying to measure up to thirty different people's ideas about what it means to be 'good with money', when we haven't even stopped to consider whether or why those opinions should mean anything to us. Often, we haven't even qualified for ourselves what having a healthy relationship with money would look like for us, and therefore become more susceptible to the opinions of others.

So, we've established that boundaries are important, but how on earth does a thoroughly unboundaried person begin to put them in place? Here, I turn again to Nedra Glover Tawwab and her invaluable book[10] for guidance, along with some other methods that I have found useful in practice. As we go through what setting or reinforcing your boundaries could look like, and how it applies to financial wellbeing, I'd suggest that you make notes whenever questions are posed, because it will give you something solid to come back to later on, and help you to follow through with your boundary setting.

The first step is to identify where boundaries are needed, or where porous boundaries might need some reinforcement. Tawwab defines porous boundaries as those that we believe that we have put in place, but fail to enforce or communicate, which can lead to feelings of resentment, and one of the examples that she gives is agreeing to loan someone money because you feel obliged to but can't actually afford to. You could extend this out to situations where you feel that you have to say yes to costly commitments, or to buy something for your children because they're nagging you, or to condone unhealthy spending behaviour from a partner because you don't want them to feel that you're judging or controlling them. Can you think of times when this applies to you, or has applied in the past? Think about all of your different relationships, both professional and personal, and make sure that you consider the other resources that can have a knock-on effect to your financial health, such as time, energy and mental capacity. Are there any relationships where you have found yourself growing resentful? Are there any people who you feel consistently ignore your boundaries?

Next, ask yourself whether you feel that you have clearly and fairly communicated those boundaries to the other person in your relationship. It could be that you have, and that the other person is ignoring or pushing back against your boundaries, in which case they need to be restated and followed through on. Speaking from experience, often when we're feeling particularly frustrated we tell ourselves or the other person that we're not going to do something again – like lending money that isn't paid back, or working an hour's unpaid overtime – but the other person assumes that it's said in the heat of the moment, and they expect the same, unboundaried behaviour from you the next time that the situation arises. This can feel like your good nature is being taken advantage of, and it damages both our relationship with the other person and our sense of self-worth. If you're in a pattern of failing to enforce your boundaries, it can feel difficult to start following through with your requests, especially if the other person is used to benefitting from your porous boundaries. Tawwab's suggestion with most boundary challenges is to stay calm and firm, but it might be helpful for you to think about the situations where these boundary violations arise, and come up with some suitable responses that you can practise ahead of time. Calling out behaviour from those you care about can feel very confrontational, which I understand can be scary, but naming problem behaviour, such as someone testing your limits or ignoring your wishes, can really help the other person to see that they're being out of order.

After this, it's important to be consistent. Just enforcing your boundaries once or twice is not likely to be enough to see a long-lasting change in the way that you interact in your relationships, or to create that protective ring around your resources that's essential to both your financial wellbeing and your general sense of happiness and self-esteem. If you allow your boundaries to lapse, or once again become porous, it can be confusing for the other person in the relationship, and your self-worth will once again start to become worn away as your resources deplete.

If this section resonates particularly with you, I highly recommend *Set Boundaries, Find Peace* as further reading. Now, though, it's time to think about what boundaries can mean for us in terms of money. My reluctance to set financial boundaries has always stemmed from a viewpoint that 'it's only money', and that it's not possible to put a price on the happiness of those I care about. However, this changes when you accept the fact that money is not just notes and coins, but a wellbeing currency in our own lives. We have to ensure that we respect ourselves enough to protect ourselves from being completely drained by those around us, or being so heavily influenced by external opinions that we forget what's important to us. We explored people-pleasing and misconceptions around generosity in the previous two sections, and you might like to bring all of this insight together for a moment of reflection around money, your relationships and your self-worth. Jot down any lightning bolts, and I'll meet you in the next section.

How to set boundaries in your relationship with money

There are certain areas of your relationship with money where porous or non-existent boundaries can cost you a lot of cash, and your peace of mind. Some of these, such as struggling to say no to expensive plans, we've covered, but here are a few more places where it's common to struggle with boundaries:

- Agreeing to work for free, or for less than you're worth.
- Lending money to others when you can't afford it, or it will impede your financial goals.
- Allowing others' opinions of you to influence your behaviour with money.

- Allowing your partner or a family member to have too much control over your finances (though this can be due to financial abuse, in which case it is *not* your lack of boundaries that are the problem).
- Feeling unable to say no to work because you're anxious that you'll need the money later.

Think about whether any of these apply to you, or if there is some other way in which a lack of boundaries is damaging your relationship with money, because the first stage of setting a boundary is identifying why you need it, and where it needs to go – like a fence. Next, you need to start enforcing the boundary, which may not be easy. Some ways to enforce your new boundary are:

Make sure that you have the vocabulary to communicate your boundary effectively but politely

The essence of this is saying 'no', but often a little more context is needed for the person to understand that you are serious, and that you're not upset with them or being rude. Try phrases like:

- I'm sorry, that's not in my budget right now. Maybe next month.
- I can't afford that right now, but thank you for asking me.
- I'm sorry but I don't have the money to help you out right now, is there another way that I can support you?
- I'm not sure you entirely understand my circumstances –

rest assured that I've done my research and am making the right decisions for me at this time.

- I don't have the capacity for unpaid work at the moment, unfortunately. If circumstances change and you're able to offer a fee, please get in touch.

Anticipate some push back, and have a response prepared

When you put in a new boundary, not everyone will understand or accept to begin with, especially if you've struggled to say no in the past – think Hannah Horvath's parents cutting her off financially in the opening episode of *Girls*, and the outrage that she reacts with. Similarly, you might consider that if a person you are close to were to change their boundaries with you, you might be resistant to the altered dynamic, at least to begin with. Try to respond neutrally and firmly, rather than getting upset that the other person is not respecting your boundary – this can be hard if you struggled to enforce the boundary in the first place, but it's important not to undo that hard work now. Try phrases like:

- I did already give you an answer, and it was no. I'm sorry if that wasn't the answer you wanted to hear, but it is final.
- As I told you, it's not affordable for me right now.
- Please respect my original answer.
- I thought carefully about my decision, so please respect it.

Try not to succumb to pressure or feelings of guilt

If you're used to pleasing others at any cost to your own wellbeing, you may feel that you are letting them down, or you may bend under pressure and end up agreeing to something very similar to the thing that you said no to. The other person may feel annoyed with you for putting your boundary in place, but this is very likely to be fleeting. If the relationship is worth maintaining, they will come to understand why your boundary is important. They may also feel that they can find a way round your boundary, by suggesting a 'lighter' version of their original request, but it's important to stay firm if this is still not something that works for you.

Prepare to be consistent

When it comes to creating firm and rooted boundaries, consistency is key. You need to be prepared to repeat this boundaried behaviour until other parties understand where that boundary is, and stop trying to step over it. If it helps, create a list of stock phrases that work in different areas – some for work, some for personal relationships – and simply repeat when needed. Having prepared responses helps to remove some of the anxiety and emotion from these exchanges. As you see the positive effects of your new boundaries, it will get easier and more automatic to enforce them.

How about . . . money manifesting?

Generally speaking, I am a manifesting sceptic. I recognize some of the basic principles – for example, focussing on what you want, overcoming limiting beliefs and directing your time and energy towards what serves you – to be sound, but the moment that vibrations or the universe are mentioned, I'm out. If there are crystals involved, I'm double out, and I find manifesting culture particularly problematic when promises are made around being able to manifest money. This idea has been popular for decades, with cohort after cohort of new 'gurus' or 'masters' touting the same rules, rehashed for new generations and evolving media. With the rise of social media, manifesting has found a whole new audience – and it is lucrative. According to some of those selling courses and teaching money manifestation, you actually can put a price on getting what you want, and it's usually at least a few hundred quid. In fact, one of the most concerning things about money manifesting is that, by and large, the people profiting from it are making most, if not all, of their own money from courses teaching others how to manifest money.

It's not my intention to dismiss or mock spirituality or belief, rather to advocate for critical thought when it comes to money, because I know the damage that can be done by blindly trusting that everything will be okay. Of course, if something is working for you as a way of addressing your feelings about your worth, it's important to respect and nurture that – financial wellbeing is a holistic concept that acknowledges that there is far more at play in our relationship with money than just the nuts and bolts of finance. If you are someone who struggles to feel deserving of money, whether that's because you feel you've failed to manage it in the past, or because you've never had enough, it's vital to overcome that in order to achieve a peaceful relationship with your finances, and to feel confident in asking to be paid your worth and comfortable with earning more. But that's not the universe – that's *you*. *You*, putting in the work to achieve financial wellbeing. *You* get to take the credit. It's important to remember that spending as though you are already wealthy, or leaving a fiver on the tube in the hope that more money will be returned to you by the universe, is not likely to help you to address the complexities of your relationship with money. The work that most people need to do around self-worth and money goes much deeper.

Money isn't the goal, it's the tool

> 'It's true that earning less [than the average annual income per capita] can dampen your sense of well-being, but earning more is not necessarily going to make you happier.'
>
> Mo Gawdat, *Solve for Happy*[11]

One of the key elements of financial wellbeing is not placing the burden of your happiness solely on your money. As we learned earlier in this step, that hedonic treadmill will keep telling us that we need more and more to be happy, and if we make goals out of arbitrary amounts of money or certain material possessions, it will never seem enough by the time we get there. So, how do we change the way that we view money, after a lifetime of being told that the ultimate goal can be quantified in the form of a certain salary or amassed wealth?

In my experience, the only thing that works is to shift our focus from monetary amounts to life situations, and then work backwards to figure out how much money we need to earn, save or invest to achieve that lifestyle. When we spoke, Anna Codrea-Rado framed this as 'lifestyle design', something that she says isn't taught to us early enough in life – and I agree. For those of us who are not independently wealthy, if we want to achieve a sense of financial wellbeing, it's absolutely essential for our earning potential in our jobs and our plans for our lifestyle to complement one another. In fact, according to Mo Gawdat's happiness equation, it's more or less vital for general happiness. The formula for happiness that he proposes in international bestseller *Solve for Happy* is that your happiness is equal to or greater than your perception of the events in your life minus your expectations of how life should behave. Positioned by Gawdat as an alternative to the complex and unending musings on human happiness by philosophers and psychologists, this simple equation is something that we can pull ourselves back to every time we can't work out why we don't yet feel satisfied with our lives. I'm always sceptical about anything that claims to reduce something as complex as happiness and wellbeing to a single line of text, but there's so much scope for adaption and expansion in this equation that it doesn't *feel* reductive. It feels like a useful tape measure, a guideline for addressing the deeper issues in our relationship with money and self. Gawdat himself explains how, even with all of the material wealth he could ever wish for, even with a wonderful partner and two perfect children, even with a prestigious job title and huge career success, he spent years of his life incredibly depressed. Every time he would get a new 'toy' – a supercar or an innovative gadget – and the happiness would be so fleeting that he would barely register it. The depression endured even as his home filled with extravagant purchases. Money and possessions were not the answer.

This is fairly well documented, both statistically and anecdotally, and something that I've reflected on myself since seeing such a huge change in my circumstances in a relatively short amount of time. While there's no doubt that the *absence* of pressing financial stress and *reduction* of financial shame have had a material impact on my happiness in that they have removed something that was actively causing me distress and impacting my mental health in a very negative way, having more money available has not magically solved all of my problems. It has not automatically made me feel like a more worthy and fulfilled person, nor has having more cash magically solved any of the issues in my relationship with money. What it has done is given me space to breathe. It's given me more freedom and better options – but it's up to me to decide what to do with that freedom and those options.

I asked my Instagram audience recently about why they wanted more money. It seems quite a basic question, but I largely find that the assumption in society is that, if offered more money without any sort of significant sacrifice, most people would say yes. I wanted to tap into people's motivations and get an idea of any recurrent themes or motivations as to why people pursue extra income or more wealth. The answers, though not surprising at all, were at odds with the spending and consumption behaviours that most of us exhibit in our daily lives. Most responses centred around freedom and security, which I've found tend to go hand in hand, even though we might associate freedom with spontaneity and security with routine. Almost everyone, aside from a woman who wanted to be able to buy more outfits for her dog without being judged by her partner (one of my favourite ever responses), had some sort of simple, longer-term, non-material purpose to their wish for more available funds. Many answers stated that they would like to feel more relaxed about money, some wanted to save for a house – having somewhere safe to live being fairly high up in Abraham H. Maslow's hierarchy – while others expressed a wish to travel more, be able to save for their children, clear debt and afford further education or a new career. All of these are related to wellbeing, happiness and fulfilment in a way that the pursuit of material wealth and possessions is not, and yet we consistently see, and ourselves participate in, financial behaviour that sabotages our goals. This isn't a judgement, or even tough love, but simply an observation that I've made time and time again in my own relationship with money and that of others. It's indicative of a need to connect what we repeatedly do with our progress towards our goals, and also how we feel, which leads us neatly on to Step Three, which is all about creating rituals and habits around money.

Concluding thoughts for Step Two

I really hope that this second step has helped you to think differently about how your finances relate to your self-worth, and what areas you need to work on to try to draw a line between the two. It's so easy to over-simplify this relationship, but in expanding our viewpoint to cover other areas, such as work and relationships, and how these feed into the relationship between our money and our self-worth, we start to feel more able to understand and then resolve them. There's a reason why I say that changing your relationship with money can change your whole life, and this step – learning and accepting that your worth stands independently of your financial status, setting boundaries and stepping off that hedonic treadmill are things that will trickle (or maybe even flow freely) into other areas of your life – is so key in that it's inevitable.

To complete this step, I'd like you to think about why money is important to you – why you want more of it, and why you want to find a sense of peace in your relationship with it.

Consider whether these are material things, or things that can be bought with cash, or whether there are other things that you want to work on too. Figure out the role that you want money to play in your life now, and in your future, and you're well on your way to a better sense of financial wellbeing. I'll meet you in Step Three.

Actions for Step Two

- ☐ Let go of your ideas about how 'good' or 'bad' you are with money.
- ☐ Identify where setting boundaries will allow you to find financial wellbeing more easily.
- ☐ Communicate those boundaries to the people who need to be made aware, reinforcing them if and when necessary.
- ☐ Reframe your ideas about generosity – it's not always about a gift or expensive gesture.
- ☐ Learn to understand, accept and overcome your feelings of envy.
- ☐ Start to see money as a tool, not the end goal.

Step Three

Creating money habits and rituals

We were inevitably going to have to move on to some practical stuff eventually, but I really want you to bring the awareness and the holistic attitude that we've covered in the first two steps into this new phase. Creating money rituals is not really as fluffy as it sounds; there are absolutely no crystals involved, for starters. I won't mention the universe once, I promise. It's about building a connection between you and your money that fosters and encourages positive habits, converting the inner work that we've been doing into measurable outcomes.

Creating routines, rituals and habits around your practice with money will support your journey towards a healthier money mindset and give you a framework for managing your money so that you don't have to think about it all the time. What most people find difficult about being financially disciplined, organized and aware is not the initial setup, but the fact that it can feel relentless and never-ending. With money, it often feels like there is always some new urgent or unexpected expense, always a new hill to climb. But if you put the right systems and habits into place, navigating these undulations in your financial circumstances will feel easier, because you'll have something to hold you. You won't feel like you're going into freefall every time money is a challenge, nor will you be lost for ideas if a little extra money comes into your life.

I find there is a common theme across every 'method' for improving your life, whether it's a tidying technique, mindfulness exercise or way of eating, which is that most life-changing things are *habits*, rather than events. They require repetition in order to make a lasting difference, and there's no quick or single fix. It's the same for looking after your financial wellbeing – once you've done the deeper work on your mindset and overcoming limiting beliefs about your ability to successfully manage your money, the magic lies in how you make it happen. How you continue to show up for yourself when it comes to money.

Creating lasting money habits and rituals

I try not to spend too much time dwelling on the practicalities of budget-building because a) there are so many free templates and guides out there and b) the hard part is actually maintaining it or 'sticking to it'. A lot of the language that we use around money and budgeting is similar to how we talk about food and dieting, with discipline held in the highest regard and any deviation from 'ideal' treated as game-changing or deal-breaking. Serial budgeters tend to apply the same all-or-nothing application to finances as yo-yo dieters do to food and exercise. Once you're in that mindset of perfection or bust, it can be really difficult to actually be fair and reasonable in your expectations of yourself. Unless you're budgeting for a very, very short-term goal, your setup should honour the fact that you – nobody else but you – are going to have to live with this. It should be liveable with and leave room for enjoyment, and that is what will allow you to build consistency and momentum in your journey, eventually leading you to achieve your financial goals and have a better relationship with money.

It's broadly acknowledged that it is what we repeatedly do that builds our world and our experience of life, rather than single events, and this relentless nature of the life admin and self-care tasks that we have to complete is what can lead us to feel burned out and despondent, which can, in turn, lead to the 'fuck it' mentality that precedes giving up. This is especially true of money management, so we have to find ways and strategies for making those repeated actions easier and incorporating them into our lives in a way that doesn't drain us. Even when we frame taking care of our finances as wellbeing practice, it doesn't mean that it always happens easily or organically, which is where the rituals and routines that we develop in this step will help to keep us engaged and on track.

Habit change – either breaking bad ones or building new ones – is difficult, and has been the subject of much discussion for decades. There are people who swear that there's a set timeframe for making and breaking habits, others who swear by methods like hypnotherapy, still others who claim to have some kind of magic formula, but the breakaway bible for habit change in the last few years is undoubtedly James Clear's *Atomic Habits*.[1] His ideas around breaking old habits and building better ones are based around making changes in tiny increments, rather than pushing for huge, unsustainable changes right from the offset. He also has some set methods for building and breaking habits that can be applied beautifully to looking after your financial wellbeing.

His basic principles, as well as building on small changes, revolve around tuning your brain to reject the old habit and embrace the new, using practical and mindset techniques. He advocates making habits that you want to phase out **invisible**, **unattractive**, **difficult** and **unsatisfying**, while making the habits that you want to adopt **obvious**, **attractive**, **easy** and **satisfying**. So, let's talk about how we can apply some of these methods to financial wellbeing.

Think about some undesirable or damaging money habits that you want to break. This could be things like overspending each month or dipping into your savings, or they could be more deeply associated with your financial wellbeing, such as feeling guilty if you spend on non-essentials or spending more than you can afford in order to please people. Making these habits **invisible** could mean removing shopping apps from your devices, or putting savings in an account that doesn't allow immediate withdrawals. Making them **unattractive** could mean pinning a list of the benefits of avoiding these habits to your noticeboard, or setting it as the background on your phone. Making them **difficult** could mean removing payment information from your devices, or setting a phone curfew to reduce late evening scrolling and shopping. To make habits feel **unsatisfying**, Clear advocates strongly for finding an accountability partner, which is something that I've seen work well with money, as well as with other healthy habits. I have a couple of people who I speak to regularly about both my personal and business finances, and it helps me to keep a sharp focus on both the future I'm trying to build and the habits that I don't want to slip back into. We've discussed the benefits of talking about money more openly and honestly, and this is one of the huge advantages – being able to find someone who feels the same way about money as you do, who will let you know if you start to veer off course, who you can talk to if you feel old habits calling.

Exercise: Create your habit-breaking toolkit

It's a great idea now to write a list of some of the habits and behaviours that you feel are damaging your financial wellbeing – you might want to look through any notes you've already made for clues if you're struggling. Then, under each one, write down some ideas for each of the four methods of breaking them – this is the beginnings of a little toolkit for breaking the money habits that are keeping you stuck.

Now it's time to think about the new habits that you'd like to put in place. These are the healthy things that you want to introduce in order to make looking after your financial wellbeing easier, and I've set out five suggested areas to work on later in this section.

First, can you think of ways to make them **obvious**? How about keeping your budget spreadsheet in a folder on your phone, or using an app-based savings account? Clear talks about designing your environment to make the positive choices the easiest ones – is this something you can look at doing spatially or digitally?

The next thing to think about is making your new habits **attractive**. This is where creating rituals, or, as Clear terms it, 'temptation bundling' comes in. When I talk about incorporating budgeting or other money management techniques into your self-care by coupling them with other, more appealing activities, I often see a little metaphorical light bulb flicker on. I'd realized fairly early in my own journey with money that if I paired updating my budget with something that I really enjoy doing, like having a long bath, or a glass of wine, or splitting a tub of Haagen Dazs with my husband, I found it much easier to do consistently. I also found that if I made this into a little Sunday-night ritual, and did it at roughly the same time each week, the knock-on effect to my wellbeing for the following week was fairly remarkable. The act of checking in with myself and creating moments of enjoyment around something that had previously terrified me gave me a sense of confidence on a Monday morning, and knowing what was coming in and what was going out that week meant that I didn't have to feel that bubbling anxiety about unexpected bills and bouncing direct debits. In the beginning, I sometimes had to push myself to open the spreadsheet and sit down, but eventually it became something that I started looking forward to. It's a method that I've expanded out into other areas too – such as saving my favourite podcasts for when I have to force myself to wash up, or watching *New Girl* for the thousandth time while I fold the laundry. Lots of these things that fall under the umbrella of 'life admin', such as money management and household chores, are actually base-level self-care, but that doesn't mean that they're exciting, or that having something to sweeten the deal won't make them more enjoyable.

Can you think about some ways that you can create rituals around your own management of your finances, or any ways that you can bundle your habits to make looking after your money feel like part of your self-care? Have a think about whether there are times in the week that you could use effectively to look after yourself by creating enjoyable moments that are actually also positively contributing to your financial wellbeing.

In terms of making your new habits **easy**, Clear's suggestions are very aligned with things that we've already covered, such as simplifying, streamlining and automating, also applying his titular principle of scaling down these desirable habits so that they can be done more quickly or with less effort in order to solidify the habit, before gradually scaling up. A good example of this could be setting up a standing order to your savings account for a very small amount of money in order to create the habit, and then increasing the amount as you make other positive changes and have more money to save.

Lastly, we need to make our new money habits **satisfying**. This one can feel tricky for a few different reasons, the first being that, with money, often the satisfying feeling really doesn't occur naturally until a little further down the line, when you begin to see the fruits of your efforts – whether that's seeing the cash stack up in your savings or a significant reduction in debt. This is where we need to find manual rewards for executing our new habits – but rewarding ourselves is often associated with spending money, which might be one of the habits we're trying to break, so we have to find other ways to light up that reward centre in our brains. Before I'd even heard of James Clear and his methods, I used a 100-square grid to track my progress out of debt, colouring in a square every time I paid off 1% of the total that I owed, and I found it incredibly motivating and rewarding. Perhaps you could do something similar, or look at other ways of tracking your progress that also feel rewarding? You can also consider using small material rewards, such a new lipstick or book, for milestones along the way to financial wellbeing, remembering to celebrate those non-tangible wins, such as enforcing boundaries, as well as monetary ones.

Another reason that it can be hard to derive satisfaction from good financial habits is that, as we've discussed, we can have a tendency to assume that having a good relationship with money and looking after ourselves financially is 'the norm', and that we don't deserve congratulating for it. But, as I hope you've come to realize, that really isn't the case for a lot of people. We all deserve to gain real satisfaction from practising financial self-care, because, against a tidal wave of pressure to borrow and consume, it can actually be really, really difficult.

Exercise: Find an accountability buddy

As you start to break the habits that are holding you back, and form new ones that will propel you forwards, an accountability partner will be invaluable in keeping you on track. We're so used to holding our financial cards close to our chest, because of the stigma and shame that surround money, that it can be really difficult to find somebody that you trust enough to partner up with – but it's so worth it. Your first port of call might be friends and family, and if there's someone inside that sphere who you feel comfortable talking to about money, that's brilliant. Otherwise, this is an area where social media can be brilliantly helpful. There are growing online communities, including my own Instagram page, where honest conversation about money is the order of the day – and you might find a like-minded person to buddy up with. Often, it's easier for someone who's not too close to you to hold you accountable, and vice versa – plus, it can be easier to be open about your challenges and mistakes with a relative stranger than with someone who knows you inside out. It's up to you to figure out what will suit you best.

Whoever your accountability buddy might be, the first thing that you'll need to do is have an initial chat to share your goals and the habits you'd like to form (and break) with one another. You will each take note of your own goals, and the other person's, and then set regular catch-ups to ensure that you're each staying on track. A good accountability buddy should be:

- Firm, but fair
- Not enabling of destructive behaviour
- Able to listen and discuss slip-ups without judgement
- Help you to work through hurdles and stumbling blocks
- Trustworthy and discreet
- Reliable
- Not in direct competition with you

This list will give you an idea of what to look for in your partner, but it also lets you know how to be a good partner in return, because this is a symbiotic relationship. You can either have a time-limited partnership that centres around a specific goal, such as saving a house deposit or for retirement, or you can choose an ongoing partnership that flows along with your goals and circumstances. The important thing to remember is that the relationship should be beneficial for you.

Personally speaking, there are a few habits and rituals that I've found to be key to building a lasting sense of financial wellbeing, and they are:

- Living with a budget
- Checking your bank balance regularly
- Consistently saving *something*
- Staying on top of debt
- Practising gratitude

This isn't a prescription, but a good baseline framework for a healthy relationship with money. If you can develop habits and rituals around these five areas, I promise that you'll see an improvement in your financial wellbeing.

Living with a budget

One day, someone will probably propose a way of having a great relationship with money without mentioning the word 'budget', but today is not that day. For me, creating a budget that actually worked with my own lifestyle and goals was transformative, but it didn't happen right away. When I was looking to turn a difficult financial situation around, not all of my motivation for budgeting came from a good place – as well as looking to make changes in how I was managing my money, I was also, I think, looking for a way to punish myself for my past mistakes. I hadn't completed the first couple of steps in this process at that point – in fact, I hadn't even really considered that there was more to do than fix the superficial elements of my finances. This was not really the right approach, and I made a lot of mistakes in those early days, being super-restrictive and setting unrealistic goals that made me feel like I was failing.

The issue was that my budgeting technique was, essentially, coming from a place of self-loathing. I hadn't made peace with my mistakes, and every ounce of my self-worth was tied to the £27,000-ish of personal debt that I'd accrued. There was a punitive aspect to it, which we commonly see in diet culture, an aspect of 'making up for' something. Before we get into the more practical elements of budgeting, which is really very simple, I'd like you to ask yourself: what are you trying to make up for? Are you going into this from a place of kindness towards yourself? Hopefully, after the first two steps, you are starting to better understand your relationship with money, and are working towards a more compassionate approach to your financial past and self-worth. You should also now have a better idea of *why* you want to make these changes, beyond just having more money, which will help you when shaping your budget.

The important thing is to reframe how you see budgeting. You might be used to seeing it as a way to punish or chastise yourself, or as something that's too time-consuming or complicated, or just not 'for you'. But it doesn't have to be any of those things, and it really is for everyone, I promise. Incorporating it into your lifestyle as one of the most important ways that you look after yourself is something that will incrementally improve and maintain your financial wellbeing through the ups and downs of life, and fluctuations in your income and outgoings. Like any other relationship, it's important that you feel *safe* in your relationship with money, and having a steady, well-maintained budget will afford you that feeling of control and security. Your budget isn't something that exists to restrict you, it should simply be an Excel manifestation of your control over your finances.

Exercise: Looking at where your budget has gone wrong

Because it's likely that you've had a least one stab at budgeting in the past, the first thing I'd like you to do is to think about the methods that you've used before, and where you think you went wrong, or where they failed to meet your needs. Don't be tempted to focus on the failure aspect – we've all started things that we didn't finish, after all – rather, think about why you weren't able to live with that budget. Was it too vague? Too restrictive? Too complicated? Take some time to think about it, and make a list of things to avoid this time round.

Exercise: Uncover your sleep-spending habits

The second exercise I'd like you to do is to take a piece of paper and draw a vertical line down the middle. Now, on one side, I'd like you to list your income – either individual or household, however you'll being doing your budget, and on the other, your outgoings. But I *don't* want you to check your bank account or any budgeting tools that you might use – do it off the top of your head. Run the totals, and see how they balance. Take a few moments to think about how you feel about that – does it reflect what tends to happen month by month, or is there a discrepancy? Does it all seem to tally in theory but, somehow, you're left with way too much month at the end of the money in practice? Now, I want you to go through your previous month's actual income and outgoings on your banking app or on your statements, and add any extra bits in a different colour. Always taking a mindful, judgement-free approach to this practice, consider the things that you missed, and how much 'sleep-spending' you're doing – those little bills and subscriptions that you forget about, the small purchases that really add up. The purpose of this exercise is to help you to realize how connected you are to your money habits, and how much you stand to gain by taking control of your financial wellbeing and creating lasting habits and rituals. It will really help later in this step, when you start to build a budget that's tailor-made for you.

The role of your budget in your wider financial wellbeing practice is, quite simply, to present you with the information that you need to set your priorities and make informed choices. For most of us, it's not possible to have it all, all at once, so we need to learn to make smart choices according to what we want and need, and what we can afford – and this is what your budget will tell you.

Making a budget that works for you

Once you have a clear view of all of the information that you need, it's time to build a budget that you can actually stick to – one that you won't avoid looking at after a couple of weeks because you can't remember how it works or you feel guilty after overspending. Your budget is the red thread running through all of your finances; the sourcebook for all of your decision-making when it comes to money. Sympathetically created and properly maintained, it can be your best friend, rather than an arduous chore or a stick to beat yourself with.

A simple budget is really just a balance sheet of your income vs your outgoings, and most are split by month, because regardless of our income schedule, major bills tend to be paid on a monthly basis. You might choose to do yours on paper, on an Excel spreadsheet or using an app, depending on what works for you, but there are a few things that your budget should be, regardless of the format.

A successful budget is:

- Easy to follow (don't give columns weird labels)
- At least a little flexible (if the Eiffel Tower didn't bend a little in the wind, it would break)
- Comprehensive (don't leave any payments or accounts out)
- Accurate (don't guess or round amounts down)

You might also choose to keep expenses in your budget, especially if you use an app that links to your bank account or a Google sheet that lives on your phone, so you can add things as you go. This is great for staying accountable and reducing 'sleep-spending' throughout the month, but can be anxiety-inducing if your issues with money revolve around needing to control every last penny and struggling to let go. This is completely up to you, but what I'd like you to do now is make your budget, or revisit an abandoned one, and look at what you need to change to make it work for you.

As you start to build your budget, carefully considering your priorities and what you feel are reasonable amounts to allocate to various different things, I'd like you to try practising a little bit of foresight. When we create our budgets, we're often in a very motivated, determined frame of mind, which is obviously great – but I'd like you to consider how easy or hard your budget might be to engage with when you have a lot on your plate, or when you're going through a period of high anxiety or low mood. Make sure that you're building something with some sway, and with compassion for your future self.

If you're not sure where to start with the practical stuff, you can download a simple, easy-to-adapt budget template for Excel and Google Sheets at www.thefwforum.com/resources/.

Checking your bank balance regularly

One of the challenges to financial wellbeing that arises again and again is the tendency to bury our heads in the sand when it comes to money. I did this for years, and while the immediate threat of what was going on with my finances was mostly neutralized, the anxiety continued to bubble away under the surface as the actual material problems grew in the dark. I was in the habit of ignoring things until they got too big and conspicuous to bypass, and then I would deal with them as quickly and superficially as I could before returning my head resolutely to the sand. A 2018 study by NS&I about money and wellbeing suggests that this isn't particularly un-common – in fact, almost three quarters (73%) who said that they worried about money also said that they had never sought advice or guidance.[2] I see this anecdotally in my work too – people often speak about being too terrified to engage with their finances, especially when they fear that things aren't going well or according to plan. It's probably one of the major stumbling blocks when it comes to financial wellbeing and, as with everything else in this step, it's something that needs constant practice.

Once you have your budget, which is, in a lot of ways, the keystone for your financial habits, it's important that you check in with it, and also with the bank account or accounts that it relates to at regular intervals. This could be daily, weekly or monthly, according to what suits you, but if you're used to avoidance tactics when it comes to money, something more regular will help you to get used to feeling connected and engaged with your finances in a healthy way. This is where exposure therapy tactics can be really useful.

Formally, exposure therapy is a form of cognitive behavioural therapy (CBT) that's usually used for treating phobias, obsessive compulsive disorder and anxiety,[3] and it's carried out by a psychotherapist or specialized practitioner. What we are talking about here, though, is using some of the techniques and principles to make facing your finances easier if you experience high levels of anxiety around money – so that the inclination to bury your head in the sand becomes weaker, and you can engage with your finances in a more relaxed and controlled way.

If your anxiety around money is causing you to avoid observing or making decisions about your finances, then the first step is to put regular checking into place. Earlier, I talked about the importance of exposing yourself to all of your financial information, and this is an expansion of that – consider how painful or anxiety-inducing that first big step was, and remember that the only way to avoid those tensions and worries building up again is to remain consistently engaged. Because we don't want to go too far in the other direction, I would suggest that checking your balances and budget once per day is sufficient to get the benefits of exposure without accidentally introducing a new compulsion to check your bank account every five minutes 'just in case', because that's not good for your financial wellbeing either. You should find that, after a few days, the little jolt of anxiety that you feel as you open your banking app starts to grow quieter and maybe even subsides, while you'll also start to feel more confident and relaxed when tapping your debit card at the checkout or even talking about money with friends. Exposing yourself to your financial situation repeatedly will help you to take ownership of it and, eventually, make you feel more empowered to change it if and when you want or need to.

Where this practice really comes into its own, but also where it is most challenging, is those times when things don't go perfectly. If you can continue practicing this engagement with your finances even during and after a period of overspending

– which does and will happen – or taking your eye off the ball, it will pay you dividends in both a practical sense and a mindset sense. It's all too common to engage enthusiastically while we feel that we're smashing it, but to panic and avoid when we feel like we've taken a wrong turn. This is a challenge that you are absolutely equal to, and one that will help you to even out your feelings about money in the long term.

In these moments, remember that acts of overspending or budgeting fails don't define you – they're just part of being human. You can return to Step One and some of the self-forgiveness practice if you need or want to, but the main thing is to stay engaged. Check your bank balance even after a bank holiday weekend when your pockets are stuffed with receipts, and you feel that swirling anxiety begin to grow. Things may not be as bad as you think they are, and even if they are, now is the time to address and put strategies into place to cope and compensate.

As time goes on, your relationship with money will grow more resilient to these challenges, and you'll find it easier to practice exposure and engagement without the accompanying stress – you just have to make it a habit, and not allow slip ups to derail your progress or your mindset.

Consistently saving *something*

Rituals and habits are king when it comes to most things around money, because it's the small actions that you take every day that add up to your bigger picture, but they are particularly critical with saving. Saving money can feel like the most positive, nourishing habit if you're doing it well – but it can also feel like an insurmountable mountain to climb if you're not used to it, or a huge amount of pressure if you get a little bit obsessed with stashing as much cash as possible. The amount that you would need to save for a house deposit, or to buy a car outright, or even to fund a big holiday, and the amount of time that it will take you to get there can feel daunting, and cause you to feel despondent, wondering what the point in trying is. But if you can reframe saving as something that you do to look after your financial health, and something that you are growing, it will make forming those habits easier to do.

Despite the fact that many of us think that we can't afford to save, and so we put it off for a future time when we might be earning more or forking out less for things like childcare, for those earning a living wage, there is usually *something* that can be put aside, even if it's just a small amount. If you can create a saving habit for a small, affordable amount each week or month – even if it's £10, to start with – you are telling yourself that saving is a priority for you, and you'll be more likely to consider stashing any spare cash in the future, rather than spending it right away. Seeing that pot of money grow, even if it's very slowly at first, is motivating, and it pushes you to take further positive actions with your money. Here are a few ways that you could start saving from scratch, making things as easy as possible for yourself:

- Use an auto-saving app, which siphons off small amounts of cash every few days without you even needing to do anything.
- Set up a small standing order for on or shortly after your payday, into a simple saving account or pot.
- Use round-ups on your spending or current account.

If you can really savour the moment when you transfer your money into your savings or, if you allow yourself to feel a rush of happiness when you get an auto-saving notification, you will start to build a connection to that positive habit. Take a moment to feel grateful that you're able to put that money away for the future, and to appreciate the fact that you are prioritizing your financial wellbeing over temporary temptations and fleeting wants.

As with all of your financial rituals and habits, you should save in a way that works for you. The last thing that you want is to over-save, and find yourself needing to withdraw money from your savings mid-month, especially if it happens frequently. There's nothing wrong with being ambitious in how much you put aside, but make sure that you're not creating a situation that will undermine your new habit by forcing you to 'undo' some of your good work before you get to feel the benefit of your savings. It's also important to link your saving habit to your budgeting habit, so that you can clearly see what you can afford to save, and where you can make changes to your spending in order to save more. A habit that works for lots of people – especially those who struggle with saving motivation or those who constantly worry that they're not saving 'enough' – is to give your savings a purpose. If you're saving for multiple goals, try creating different saving accounts or pots and labelling them – i.e. 'Emergency Fund', 'Holiday', 'House Deposit', 'Christmas'. We'll talk a little more about this in Step Five.

Exercise: Get started with saving

If you've never found yourself able to save, there are a few things that you can to do make it easier for yourself:

- The first thing that you'll need to do is to review your budget, and work out the monthly or weekly amount that you'd like to begin saving – it bears repeating that this should be an achievable amount, which you can always increase in the future, once you've established the habit.
- Set up a standing order with your bank for the amount that you've calculated.
- Try to set up your transfer date for the day you get paid or the one after, if you get paid a weekly or monthly salary.

- Review your saving amount every few months, to make sure it's still the right amount. You could also review it any time your circumstances change, such as if you get a pay rise, or if you lose out on income.

Complete all of these steps and, ta-da! You're now a saver!

Staying on top of debt

Credit and debt are, in themselves, nothing to be afraid of, but keeping debt under control is vital for your financial wellbeing. My experience with out-of-control debt made a positive relationship with money feel completely out of reach, especially as I had no savings or financial safety net. Having problem debt – which we can loosely define as debt that is affecting your mental health, or where the repayments are really affecting your ability to manage day-to-day and month-to-month – can make you feel like you're constantly on the back foot, or treading water with no hope of actually being able to swim in the direction that you want to go. If at all possible, this type of debt is probably best avoided altogether, but please be reassured that even if you do have significant debt, it's entirely possible to pay it back and start building something in the other direction, whether through budgeting and patience or, if you're struggling to make repayments, with the help of a debt organization.

Keeping debt under control, like most things, is much easier when you make a habit of it. Even for people who consider themselves 'good with money', it's very easy to overspend on a credit card, because it's one step removed from your everyday finances. There's often a delay in the payment being visible on your account, it won't immediately affect your current account budget and you get to experience the pleasure of buying something without also experiencing the pain of paying for it right away. There's a disconnect between our spending behaviour and the financial consequences, which can really distort our ideas about what we can afford to spend, and leave us spiralling into financial difficulty if we're not careful.

Successfully managing debt and credit accounts is, in theory, very simple, but it can be harder in practice, when life and emotions get in the way. There's still a lot of stigma attached to most kinds of debt that can make it more difficult for us to engage with our debt in a positive and proactive way. The more we want to sweep it under the carpet, the more afraid we are to look at it head-on, the harder we make it to develop good habits around it. I really hope that completing Step Two, and doing some work around the relationship between your finances and your self-worth, will have made this a bit easier. The more we can remove emotions from decisions about credit and debt, the easier it is for us to manage them in a healthy way, because we're not bouncing from one knee-jerk reaction to another like a pinball. I know first-hand the effect that having debt can have on your mindset, and it's easy to slip into a cycle of panicking and frantically paying off as much as you can, then falling short in your monthly budget and having to borrow again. It's so hard to manage your finances in a calm and healthy way when you're acting out of fear and panic most of the time. Solid spending and repayment habits will really help you to regain control, and apply a slightly more clinical, neutral approach to managing debt.

If you use your credit card for small purchases throughout the month, which are affordable, it's a great idea to set up a direct debit to collect the full amount when you get paid – like with saving, the sooner this amount leaves your account, the more accurately you can plan your monthly finances. The danger with making payments ad-hoc is that you might get busy and miss one, while the risk with paying the minimum and letting balances run over from month to month is that the amount you owe will creep up and up, and you'll be left with an anxiety-inducing bill after a few months. It's a good idea to make a habit of checking your balance regularly, so that you don't end up with a nasty surprise six months down the line.

If you're using your credit card to spread the cost of a bigger payment, divide the amount that you owe by the number of months that you want to pay it off in, and make sure that you have a direct debit set up for that amount, also on the first of each month, or whenever you get paid. If you're self-employed without a monthly salary, it's still a really good idea to keep your payment dates consistent – having a regular structure to your outgoings does, at least, create a little bit of stability and awareness of your financial situation, and will enable you to plan.

Exercise: Make a plan for your debt

If you have debt, whether it's causing you stress and worry or not, the key to keeping it under control, and in turn ensuring that it doesn't have a negative impact on your financial wellbeing – because it really doesn't have to, no matter what anyone might tell you – is to have a plan.

If your debt is a financing plan or loan, where the term and monthly repayments are agreed at the beginning of the arrangement, your plan might be fairly simple. Just make sure you're aware of:

- What the interest rate is.
- How much your repayments are.
- When they are due to leave your account.
- When your last repayment is, and whether there's a balloon payment (this means that your final repayment is for a larger amount than your monthly payments, and is popular with things such as PCP car finance agreements).
- Where you're going to redirect that income once the term is over.

Make all of this information readily available in a spreadsheet or notebook, so that you can refer back to it.

If your debt is on a credit card or 'buy now, pay later' account, where you can keep borrowing more and the amount that you repay each month can be variable, it's much easier to get a bit lost with how much you should be repaying and when. A little more self-discipline is needed, especially if you're susceptible to emotional spending, but making your plan to pay off this kind of debt means making a commitment to limiting, or even eliminating, the use of your credit account while you're repaying the balance. Even if you intend to continue using your account after clearing your debt, which is perfectly fine, you still need a plan for reducing what you owe. Try something like this:

- Calculate how much you can afford to repay each month, making sure that you're still leaving at least a little leeway for enjoyment in your budget. Remember, punitive budgeting doesn't work long term.
- Calculate roughly how long it will take you to repay your debt if you make these repayments each month.
- If you have multiple credit accounts, prioritize them either in order of interest (i.e. how expensive the debt is) or in order of smallest to largest (so that you get those motivating wins early on). Then, focus most of your available funds on the first priority, while still

making the minimum repayments on the others.
* Track your progress in a spreadsheet or notebook to keep you motivated.

Practising gratitude

When we're looking to improve our finances, it can be tempting to skip the softer skills and habits in favour of an increased focus on the practical and number-driven elements, but it's important not to do this. If this approach worked for everyone, there would have been no need for me to write this book in the first place – these supporting practices are the mould that holds everything else in place, so don't skim over this section.

Gratitude is a habit that will likely enhance not only your relationship with money but also trickle into other areas of your life. It's easy to be sceptical about gratitude practice, especially if a difficult relationship with money and consumerism has coloured the way that you view things. For a period of my life, I found it very difficult to feel grateful for anything I had, because I was constantly looking at what everybody else had, and feeling as if I wasn't measuring up. The comparison was making me miserable, and the growing debt that I was accruing in pursuit of perfection was making me anxious, and it didn't feel like there was an awful lot to be grateful for.

I discovered the power of gratitude while I was in the thick of repaying my debt, and trying to find a way to make peace with money as I was learning to understand and control it. With most of our income going on bills and debt repayments, there was a lot of lifestyle adjusting to be done, and it was sometimes difficult not to feel resentful of the things that I felt I was missing out on. I needed to find a way to reframe the experience I was having, and gratitude gave me the ability to do that.

There are a number of studies investigating the science of gratitude and how it helps to improve mental health,[4] but it can actually be quite difficult to define what gratitude is. Here, we're talking about it as a practice – something that we actively participate in – but for most of us, gratitude is a feeling that occurs naturally under certain conditions. Psychologists Dr Robert Emmons and Dr Michael McCullough define gratitude as a two-step process: 1) 'recognizing that one has obtained a positive outcome' and 2) 'recognizing that there is an external source for this positive outcome.'[5] In my experience, both of these things require active recognition if we're to fully appreciate them, rather than relying on an innate sense of gratitude that must compete with other, louder thoughts and feelings in order for us to hear and acknowledge it. And, while it does seem that some people are naturally more able to tune into that grateful inner voice than others, the good news is that it's possible to train ourselves to listen more closely, and that the act of amplifying our gratitude could help to diminish those louder, more negative voices – especially those telling us that we don't have *enough*, that we ourselves are not *enough*. In a 2018 White Paper entitled, *The Science of Gratitude*, Summer Allen of The Greater Good Science Centre at UC Berkeley explores the evidence for gratitude as a positive force in the human experience: 'Research suggests that gratitude may be associated with many benefits for individuals, including better physical and psychological health, increased happiness and life satisfaction, decreased materialism, and more.'[6] All of these benefits, but particularly the final two, play a significant role in our financial wellbeing, and it's clear to see how mastering a gratitude habit could influence how we think and feel about money in a meaningful way.

If gratitude feels difficult sometimes, you can try using per-spective as a means to access it.

Exercise: Establish your gratitude habit

There are a few different ways that you can look to express or focus on your gratitude, and also various ways to incorporate gratitude practice into your everyday life. The frequency and form that your practice takes are up to you, but here are a few ideas to get you started:

- Start by just noticing the feeling. It doesn't have to be a huge rush: even something as simple as your partner or housemate making you a hot drink should be enough for you to pick up on. Observe, and make a mental note each time you say thank you over the course of a day.

- Keep a gratitude journal. You don't need any special kit, just a notepad and a pen, and it can take any form that you like – free or long-form writing, bullet points or just notes in margins.

- Express your gratitude to others. If the actions of another person are the source of your gratitude, make sure that they know it, and if the source of your gratitude is abstract or inanimate (for example, a beautiful walk, a moment alone or a particularly nice sandwich), tell someone else about it.

- Pair your gratitude expressions with another habit to help you to remember – such as pelvic floor exercises. You might decide to think of or say three things that you are grateful for in the shower each morning, or while you're walking your dog, or on your commute. You might even bundle gratitude with another of your financial wellbeing habits – jotting down a few things that you are grateful for before you check your bank balance or review your budget, for example, might make it easier for you to approach those tasks without fear or anxiety.

Think about whether you want to approach gratitude more as a thinking practice or as a writing practice, and give yourself the goal of performing your chosen gratitude ritual consistently for a week to begin with. Then you can make any tweaks that are needed and continue to incorporate it into your daily life going forward.

Don't over-complicate things

As someone with a lot of personal experience of over-committing myself financially, I can't emphasize the importance of this enough. There was a time when a disproportionate amount of my time and energy was spent juggling small amounts of money from one account to another, struggling to make the minimum repayments on a handful of credit cards (each with different interest rates), a store card, an overdraft and a car on finance. With so many different bills coming out at different times of the month, and a knife-edge situation in terms of balancing the totals, money was often the last thing I thought about before I went to sleep at night and the first thing on my mind when I opened my eyes in the morning. I thought about it obsessively at certain times, and forced it from my mind at others – probably as an act of self-preservation, because it's hard to maintain a constant state of heightened anxiety.

The more complicated your financial setup is, the less in control of the situation you feel, and the more tempting it becomes to bury your head in the sand to avoid the anxiety and uncertainty altogether, or at least until you're forced to face it. Whenever you make new financial decisions – whether that's taking on new debt, changing your current account, dipping a toe in the water with investing – try to keep everything as streamlined as it needs to be in order not to overwhelm you. We each have different capacities for storing and acting on information, and those capacities will tend to fluctuate over the course of our lives as we have busier and quieter periods at work, our relationships change, our caring responsibilities change etc. Part of the process of getting to know yourself and learning to trust yourself in our first couple of steps feeds into this ability to decide what setup works for you. It's really important to be honest with yourself about what you can commit to, in terms of money, time and energy.

Part of this streamlining of your finances might be to create different accounts or pockets for different purposes, taking into account interest rates, accessibility and any reward schemes. There are so many different products out there, and such a huge amount of information about each one, that you might need to take some time to properly research before committing yourself, and that's okay. Being considered and mindful in our approach to money is a very key element of financial wellbeing.

Bearing in mind the fact that most of us have a lot of other things on our minds besides money, and that this is often one of the reasons why our finances become neglected and cause problems or may just not be working as hard for us as they should be, there's something to be said for automating as much as possible and taking some of that mental load off. The digital age has made it much easier to spend beyond your means and access unaffordable credit, but it's also made it much easier to manage your finances in a positive way too. You can set up new accounts and standing orders in seconds, on the bus, if you want to. Having access to all of your accounts – even your pension in some cases – on a device that you carry with you everywhere can help you to feel in control as you navigate daily life.

If your finances are currently complex or over-committed, or entwined with someone else's, streamlining them might be a gradual process. But at this point, it's a great idea to get all of that information out in front of you, leaving no stone unturned. All of your bills, accounts, debts and assets should be completely visible to you, because it's impossible to feel happy and relaxed about money if you're not actually sure what's going where, what your interest rates are and whether your arrangements are working for you.

For some people, a simple setup would look like having one account for bills, one for disposable income and incidental expenses, one for savings and one for paying off debt, whereas other people prefer to have their money all in one place. If you share finances with a partner, you might each have a personal account plus a joint account for bills, or you might pool absolutely everything together – it's a very personal choice. It's now time, though, to decide what about your financial arrangements is or isn't working for you. If you have multiple credit cards, you could look into consolidating the debt, or closing accounts without a balance. If you have one big savings pot with no purpose, and you keep dipping into it, you might like to look at creating separate pots with different goals, which is possible with lots of banks – both traditional and challenger – nowadays.

Make sure that you stay aware of your own capacity for keeping track of things, and try to automate as much as possible if you struggle to stay on top of manually managing payments. The simplest way to do this is to create standing orders to each of your different accounts, leaving your current account shortly after you get paid. This can be trickier for self-employed people and students, who might be paid at random times of the month or in lump sums, but if you're able to create a system where your income is as consistent and steady as possible, it will help your relationship with money to be less frantic. How you structure your finances is up to you, and every person's needs are individual to them, but keeping it as simple as possible is important if you're hoping to build positive and consistent habits.

Exercise: Create a structure for your finances

Take a blank piece of paper or notebook page, and first write down all of the different places where your money exists, including current accounts, savings, debts, investments, and even perhaps your pension pots. Draw lines and arrows depicting the flow of money – i.e. from your current account to your savings etc.

Next, consider whether this setup is working for you. If it's too complex or confusing, or if you realize that some of it doesn't make sense, it might be time to look at streamlining or switching things up. Create your ideal structure and flow, and then write a list of the changes you need to make to get there.

Exercise: Create your money habit tracker

Now take some time with all of the resources that you've gained so far, and start to consider how you can incorporate new, positive financial habits into your life while minimizing or getting rid of ones that no longer serve you. Lots of journals now include a little habit tracker, or you can create your own in a notebook using the simple model below. To use it, just list your habits on the left, and then colour in or check the box when you've completed your habit:

Habit	Monday	Tuesday	Wednesday	Thursday	Friday	Saturday	Sunday

Creating a positive feedback cycle for your new habits

An important thing to consider is how these habits and rituals feed into and support one another. The nature of a positive feedback cycle means that, often, one good habit is the stepping stone to another, or acts as a motivating factor for other healthy habits, but also that allowing one habit to lapse can lead to a domino effect, whereby other positive habits start to topple too. Noticing the relationship between your financial habits, and also taking into account any other habits that you might have, and how they relate to your financial ones, is important, because it allows you to notice warning signs and act before things feel out of control.

I'll give you the example of yoga. I have been practising yoga intermittently since my mid-twenties, with periods where I attend classes two or three times a week and practise at home, and periods where I don't do a single pose or take a single deep breath for months on end. I started off seeing yoga as exercise – a way to burn calories, improve my flexibility and perhaps escape the noisy whirring inside my head for a short while. Purely practical. I was nervous the first day that I stepped into the studio, thinking that everyone else would be as slim, flexible and well-hydrated as I wished I was. I felt like I should have done some homework, some sort of preliminary course in how to participate. I would have quite liked to already be good at it before I set foot in this place that had been created in order to teach people how to do it.

I'd heard so much about the health benefits, but I was worried that I wouldn't be good enough at it, that I'd make a fool of myself. I was also slightly concerned that the class was 75 minutes long, and that I might die if I had to exercise for that long all in one go. But then the class started, and all of my worries melted away. I realized that, for all of the glowing yogis that I saw, the actual yoga practice was just one building block in a much wider journey. That those snatched sessions a few times a week were not transforming any lives on their own, but instead acted as a catalyst for healthier living in general.

I started to see the effects of this myself, in real time. The more time I spent feeling connected with my body, the better I wanted to treat it. Not by cutting out food groups or doing gruelling exercise, but by making better and more mindful choices, incrementally. It happened almost by osmosis, with more caring choices becoming easier to opt for, semi-automatic.

My relationship with my body and my relationship with money are similar in their complexity, and there have been moments where they have existed as a perfect mirror image of one another. So, as I started to work on my relationship with money, the memory of this yoga phenomenon came back to me. I realized that if there are practices that can help you to feel more connected to your body, which act as a medium for building better habits, that there might be something similar for money too.

For me, that thing is budgeting. It acts as the central hub of all of your financial activity, empowers you to make decisions and incites more thoughtful behaviour around money. And, like a gym membership or yoga pass, if your budget is left to languish in a notebook or Google drive somewhere, its magical powers stop working, and it becomes yet another thing to feel guilty about. This is why our rituals and routines around money are so important.

Coping when things don't go right

Your money habits and rituals are there as a safety net – they are designed to be the constant fixture that helps you to stay on track even when life gets really busy, or throws you curveballs. However, as we've discussed, even acts of self-care take effort to keep up, and even fully established habits require upkeep. We also know that, inevitably, when we're short on time or energy, it's often the things that we do to look after ourselves rather than other people that tend to fall off a cliff. It's amazing how quickly even the healthiest of rituals – even the ones where you can actively feel them making a difference in your life – can start to unravel if your priorities shift just a little. We tell ourselves that we can skip a check-in or two, that we'll update our budget when we have time, and before we know it it's been a few weeks and we're starting to feel rusty or out of control.

The thing that we need to make sure that we retain is perspective. Missing a few days of budget tracking or letting your bank balance get a bit out of control for a few days or weeks does not have to be a life sentence – when we apply the context of the whole of the rest of our lives, it can simply be a blip. You are going to experience times when you feel like you're failing to look after your financial wellbeing, when you take your eye off the ball and start to worry about your ability to manage your money again, but what is absolutely vital is that you don't let everything lapse. It's so easy to allow your own needs to play second fiddle to those of others, but remember that if you allow your mental, emotional and financial resources to become depleted through a lack of care and attention, the effects of that will knock on to other people anyway. So, no matter how long you've allowed those habits to lapse, no matter how much dust your budgeting spreadsheet has gathered, it is always the right choice to re-engage and carry on. And the more lapses you have, the easier it will be to push yourself back in the right direction – not that I'm advocating allowing your habits to fall away too frequently, of course.

Exercise: Write your emergency plan

The final exercise in this step is to write yourself an emergency plan – something that you can refer to when it all seems to be going completely wrong. You might include actions such as enlisting your accountability buddy for a pep talk, or writing a note from you right now to future you, to be opened in case of emergency. You could reaffirm your reasons for wanting to work towards financial wellbeing, or remind yourself of the progress you've already made. Put it in an envelope or in a folder on your computer, and forget about it until such a time as you need it.

Concluding thoughts for Step Three

So much of the progress that we make, whether in terms of our mindset, our attitude or our material circumstances, is based not in single actions or decisions that we make but in the small, inconspicuous things that we commit to doing every day. Anyone can decide to change their relationship with money or prioritize their financial wellbeing, but those who succeed in doing so will be those who manage to find a way to incorporate new practices into their everyday life, and who follow through on that commitment to fostering a more positive relationship with money. Once you learn to understand your current tendencies and patterns of behaviour, it becomes easier to break habits that are damaging your relationship with money and create new habits that will help you to repair it.

By making old habits difficult and unappealing, and taking steps to make new, desirable habits easy end enjoyable, we can create a situation whereby we are moving towards financial wellbeing without having to constantly push – some of this progress will be fuelled by the momentum that we gain from this new set of habits, all of which will support and enhance one another. In reframing practices that we might previously have considered to be a chore, or at the very least life admin, as self-care, and in savouring the moments when we make positive choices for our money, we are looking after not only our finances but our general sense of wellbeing too.

Needless to say, this step can and should be broken down into smaller increments, and you will probably find that focussing on one or two habits at a time, rather than trying to redesign your whole approach to money in one fell swoop, will prove easier and more sustainable. I hope that once you've followed the exercises and considered the reasons behind each, you will have come up with a tailor-made framework for your new relationship with money, which will help you to withstand the pull of comparison, manipulative marketing and emotional spending, which we'll discuss in more detail in Step Four. I'll meet you there as soon as you're ready.

Actions for Step Three

As the most practical step in this journey, it's important to allow yourself enough time to take some solid actions based on what we've covered in Step Three.

- ☐ Make a list of the money habits that you'd like to break.
- ☐ Make a list of new habits that you'd like to form, based around the five areas explored in Step Three.
- ☐ Get yourself an accountability partner.
- ☐ Make your old habits **invisible**, **unattractive**, **difficult** and **unsatisfying**.
- ☐ Make your new habits **visible**, **attractive**, **easy** and **satisfying**.
- ☐ Devise ways to track your habits and keep a paper trail.
- ☐ Approach your new financial habits from a self-care perspective.

Step Four

Learning to spend mindfully

> 'Consumer culture promises us that we can buy our way
> out of pain – that the reason we're sad and angry is not
> that being human hurts; it's because we don't have those
> countertops, her thighs, these jeans. This is a clever way
> to run an economy, but it's no way to run a life'
>
> Glennon Doyle, *Untamed*[1]

It's very hard to live with a budget or execute better money habits successfully if your spending is completely out of control, because no matter how well something works on paper, the numbers won't translate into your experience of life unless your real-life actions match your theoretical ones. That's not to say that there can be no room for spontaneity, only that life is easier when you are spending with intention and attention most of the time.

This is another place where external factors shoulder a lot (though not all) of the blame for our habits. In order to have a healthy relationship with spending, we have to learn to push back against a lot of outside pressure, and that can be really difficult. The whole concept of advertising and marketing is finding ways to get you to part with your cash in the most cost-effective way possible, and companies are not shy about manipulating your emotions in order to do that. Although I do have some insider knowledge of the kind of targeting that goes on, having worked in brands and marketing in a previous life, you really only have to watch a single episode of *Mad Men* to gain a basic understanding of how it all works. We are all boiling pots of emotions, ready to spew out our credit card details if tapped in the right place. I won't go as far as to say that advertising should be banned, because it is really just a by-product of the capitalist society that we live in, and is a gigantic industry in itself, employing a lot of people and putting food on the table for a lot of households. But it's also a very big factor in our financial wellbeing, and we need to take it into consideration when we look more closely at our spending behaviour and what we can do to ensure that we're not being manipulated into using shopping as a way to process our emotions. Building resilience to some of the techniques used, like FOMO and comparison, as well as gaining a greater understanding of why we respond the way that we do to certain stimuli, will enable you to feel more in control of your spending and promote better financial wellbeing.

In order to make sure that we're practising mindful spending most of the time, we also need to tap into some of the internal work that we covered in Steps One and Two – the feeling of being enough without sacrificing everything to please others, not limiting our beliefs around what we can and can't achieve with money, and making sure our boundaries are present and correct. Make sure that you bring that progress with you into this step.

The omnipresent cycle, and how to break it

Emotional spending is cyclical, as with so much else about wellbeing and money. It can be hard to identify where it starts, or where we can intervene to try to redirect ourselves, but it's vital that we find a way to break those patterns of behaviour if we are hoping to develop a better relationship with money. My own journey towards control over my emotional spending habits has definitely had its ups and down, and a lot of the financial trouble I found myself in for the first decade or so of my adult life was triggered by my struggle to deal with my emotions in a healthy way, and dips in my mental health. At times when my anxiety levels have been running high, I've always reached for shopping as a release, a way to relieve some of the tension building in my brain. Similarly, when I was feeling low, or bored, or lonely, I would search for what was missing in my life and decide that whatever it was, I could probably plug the gap, at least temporarily, with a new dress or scatter cushion. It would work for a brief moment, giving me a hit of dopamine and something to look forward to. Posting pictures of the same 'it' products as everyone else on social media helped me to feel as if I was part of a club, which I found especially difficult to resist when dealing with the turbulent emotions of new motherhood, with both of my children but especially with my second son.

But it never lasted. The brief buzz of a new purchase would quickly be replaced by worry about the financial implications, and logically I should have stopped, but the worse I felt, the more I spent. I would give myself a severe talking to one day, and go straight back to browsing H&M Home the next. Buying new clothes never made me happier with how I looked, just as covering my rented home with decorative homeware never made me feel less inadequate for not owning property. I was perpetually unsatisfied, always thinking that the next product would be the one that made me feel prettier, more stylish, happier. As I started to build a community, I learned that this is far from abnormal – that it's relatively common to have a complex and unhealthy relationship with spending. And, as with everything else about this process, knowing that I wasn't alone, feeling supported and understood for the first time, helped me to find the strength that I needed to challenge the way that I was doing things.

Broadly speaking, cycles of emotional spending tend to go like this:

The Emotional Spending Cycle

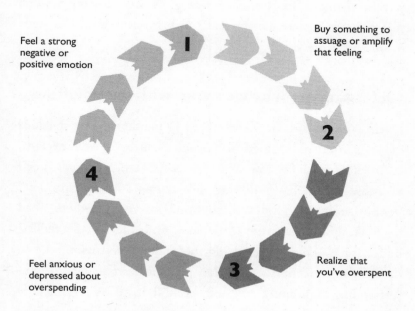

Feel a strong
negative or
positive emotion

Buy something to
assuage or amplify
that feeling

1

2

Realize that
you've overspent

3

4

Feel anxious or
depressed about
overspending

Obviously, there will be triggers and factors that are unique to you, but the process is usually similar for everyone, and similarly difficult to opt out of without doing some of the deeper work on self-worth that we've discussed. I'd like you to think about what your own triggers are – maybe look back at some of the things that you've bought and come to regret and think about the circumstances surrounding them. Think about what your own cycle looks like and how you might be able to break it using some of the practical techniques that we'll cover in this step. Make sure that you consider both how you were feeling and the external forces that were at play – is there a certain set of conditions that acts as a perfect storm for you in terms of emotional spending? Is there a deeper need that you are repeatedly ignoring and trying to shut out with more and more stuff?

Understanding why we spend with our emotions

During the first wave of the Covid-19 pandemic, the shackles of consumerism seemed to loosen a little. I saw exclamation after exclamation of 'This is amazing! I don't need all those things I was buying! I'm saving so much money!' People seemed to be waking up from the mindless need to make purchase after purchase, and they were feeling better for it. They were seeing the material results pile up in their savings accounts, and they were experiencing the corresponding lightening of their mental load. Worrying less about money, dealing with less buyer's remorse, was making people feel better.

And then the pandemic wore on, and we got tired. We experienced tough times, our homes became lethal cocktails of undiluted feelings, we missed our friends and families. We were bombarded with bad news, the rising death count ticking us through the time like a metronome, each daily briefing harder to sit through than the last. And we reached out for our usual coping mechanisms, but they weren't there. We couldn't go to the gym, or the pool, or our parents' living room. Lots of us were deprived of any sort of human touch entirely. There was nobody even to hold us through such a strange and disorientating time. We were living through a collective trauma, and we were grieving for life as we knew it, and nothing was the same.

There was one thing, though. A guaranteed dopamine hit that you only needed a smartphone, tablet or laptop to access. Online shopping. The double-high of the checkout button and doorbell ring made spending online one of the only crutches for many people, and all of those gains from earlier in the year quickly ebbed away. I wrote about this phenomenon for Refinery29, interviewing a brilliant psychologist, Dr Eleanor Seddon, who probably did more for my understanding of spending habits in a few minutes than I had gained from months of self-examination. Dr Seddon explained to me about the soothing systems that we all have in place to help us to cope with strong or difficult emotions and make us feel safe, but also about the limitations that those soothing systems have when combined with our fast-paced consumer culture.

'The problem is that our brain is hard-wired to take decisions that benefit us in the short term but may make the problem worse in the long run. Emotional spending provides an immediate sense of wellbeing. The dopamine hit of "treating yourself" is a quick way to feel better without considering the consequences that may actually make our mood worse,' she says.

'Emotional spending is perfectly normal to a degree, however it can become a "fall back" for trying to get rid of difficult emotions and only serves to create more stress in the long run. Online shopping is a particularly easy way to spend without considering the consequences because it can feel less real and delayed payment options may give a false sense of security.'

Understanding *why* we make seemingly illogical choices when it comes to spending, and why our emotions hold such sway over something that should, in many ways, be a simple maths decision, can be really helpful in creating a change in our behaviour. Appreciating the way that my brain was working at times when I was drawn to online shopping helped me to recognize that making very quick spending decisions, or feeling a pressing urge to buy expensive items, usually meant that there was something else going on, and I learned to use this feeling as a prompt to explore and interrogate those feelings, rather than succumbing to the urge (most of the time).

Now is the time to start looking at the circumstances under which you tend to shop according to impulse rather than need, and decipher why and how you end up making spending decisions that you later regret, or that you can't afford. For most of us, there will be certain triggers or series of events that lead us to seek the temporary high of an order confirmation email or the steady chug of a receipt printing behind the counter. For example, does your impulse spending tend to happen in the evening, when you're bored, anxious or lonely? Often, in the past, when I was left alone with my thoughts, or

I wanted to block out a difficult day or looming deadline, I would start to scroll social media or browse one of my favourite shopping sites. Sometimes, when we need to stop thinking for a moment, it is these old, entrenched habits that we return to, over and over – and the more time we spend scrolling, the more susceptible we are to comparison and temptation. The more 'stuff' we expose ourselves to, the more we look around our own lives and possessions and find them wanting. The more we allow our online environment to warp our perception of what we have, the less able we are to feel grateful, and the less worthy we feel.

Conversely, maybe you spend not to quieten a brain that is throwing too many thoughts your way but to feel anything at all. When we are exhausted, numb or feeling low, that burst of dopamine can give us a bit of a high without us even really considering whether we want the thing we're buying or not, a bit like the sugar rush from inhaling a pack of biscuits without really tasting them. The crash in mood (or blood sugar levels) is then more or less inevitable, and is often accompanied by frustration that the thing we did to make ourselves feel better didn't actually even work.

Exercise: Analyse past purchases

If you can start to pick apart those catalysts for any spending that isn't serving your financial wellbeing, or is getting in the way of your goals, you will have made the first step towards changing that behaviour. A good way to do this is to look through some past bank statements, or on your banking app, and pick out some purchases that you went on to regret. Write the item at the bottom of a piece of paper, and then see if you can work backwards through the circumstances surrounding that purchase, tracking the emotions that went along with it. For example, if the expense that bothered you was a takeaway that you didn't really want and hadn't budgeted for, maybe you can trace it back to feeling too exhausted to wash up or clean the kitchen, or to feeling frustrated that your partner never offers to cook, or just having a brain so busy that you couldn't even decide what you wanted.

Then, shooting off from the factors leading into that decision, make some suggestions for what you might have done differently to avoid travelling down that path. For example, could you have reinforced a boundary in asking your partner to share the cooking responsibilities with you? Could you have gone to bed earlier in order to feel more rested for today? Could you have listened to a meditation, podcast or audiobook to create some separation between your work day and your personal time?

You will never run out of things to buy

Here's the thing: you will never run out of things to buy. Our brains are hard-wired to want to finish things – it's why we continue scrolling Instagram or TikTok for hours, long after it's stopped satisfying any part of us – but you can't 'complete' shopping in the same way that you can't ever finish the scroll. There will always be a way to 'level up' your life according to some arbitrary external measure – more clothes, fancier holidays, a bougier sofa, better eyebrows. I suspect many of us are subconsciously waiting for that magical moment to come where some internal checklist of 'stuff' is completed, and we can live happily ever after. I am here to tell you that, as far as I can tell, that moment does not exist. We have to define it for ourselves.

Some of this is innate and primal, but much of it is, well, capitalism and consumerism. We are conned into thinking that 'settling' is something awful, repulsive – as though being content is the worst thing that could ever happen to us – because aspiration makes us more profitable. It's true that settling for things that are inherently not right for you, or less than you deserve, is not a good thing – especially in some areas of your life, such as a partnership where the other person is not contributing enough or a job where your salary doesn't reflect your value. Often, we accept these things when our self-esteem is low, because we don't believe we're worth more, and that's something that we have to fight. But that's not the kind of 'settling' that I'm talking about here. I'm talking about rejecting the need to constantly level up – the need to always have the latest model of something, or a bigger house, or a newer car. There is such an oversupply of stuff, such an abundance of options when it comes to consumer goods, that we will never 'complete' shopping. There isn't a big boss that you have to defeat at the end, the game just goes on and on, *ad infinitum*. Hopefully, now that you understand how hedonic adaption works, you've started to think about things that you can put into place to combat that urge to keep levelling up, but this step goes deeper into why we often over-spend and what we can do to change things.

You're allowed to want material things

This might seem like a contradiction to my point above, but stay with me. Materialism is a tricky line to walk, because there is absolutely no doubt in my mind that, while the pursuit of attaining an endless stream of increasingly expensive 'stuff' is futile and misery-inducing, sometimes material things can make life easier and more enjoyable. Beautiful – or at least comfortable – surroundings inspire creativity and contribute to our wellbeing, wearing bright colours can lift your mood, and I'm fairly sure that dishwashers save marriages. Material possessions can, to a degree, have a positive effect on our happiness, especially those that contribute to our safety – think back to that hierarchy of needs – and comfort, and those products and technologies that entertain us or the services that help us to safeguard our time. My point is that there is a limit to how much of this stuff we need before it starts making us actively unhappy, and that we must decide and impose that limit on ourselves in a world where there is an infinite amount of stuff to buy, and an ever-increasing pool of options for financing those purchases.

There's a real paradox around materialism in our culture, whereby what we can afford to buy and the lifestyle we have is deemed to be a measure of our success, but it's also often considered vulgar to covet material things. So, how can we service our desire for material things without accruing debt, clutter, or even just wasting money that we could use for other things on material possessions (that we only value up until the point that we own them)? There are a few different ways that we can manage this, all of which involve having a clear idea of the value that things hold for us, and what our priorities are.

The guidance I'd like to give first – and it was a real revelation to me when I hit upon it, even though it should be blindingly obvious – is that you can actually appreciate beautiful or appealing things without needing to own them. We're so used to being able to shop every image that we see on social media – encouraged, of course, by the retailers who are looking for ways to make absolutely everything shoppable – that we sometimes lose sight of the fact that we can appreciate a lovely living room or incredible outfit without actually needing to possess those products. The number of times that I've bought things that were of absolutely no use to me, didn't fit in my house or didn't suit my shape, just because I'd seen them looking great in another person's life doesn't bear thinking about. Can you think of any times when this has applied to you? So many of our material desires are fleeting, and easily forgotten about, even when they feel like the most important thing in the world while we are lusting after them. Sometimes, wanting something doesn't mean that we actually have to buy it – sometimes it can be a lovely, fleeting appreciation for something. Almost all of those feelings of wanting to possess something, no matter how strong they were in the moment, will pass. Like a school-age crush in both intensity and brevity, you can allow the desire for 'stuff' to wash over you, and only *buy* things when they offer you something more substantial in return for your money. Only buy things that are 'marriage material', as it were; things that you don't mind living in your house for years to come.

The second method I've found to be invaluable when it comes to wanting things is keeping a running list of things that I'd like to buy. Putting something on a list helps us to feel like we've acted on our desire for a particular item, without us actually having to make the financial commitment of buying it. It also gives us time to consider the cost, why we want it, and what the impact on our financial health will be if we do buy it. Simply writing it down rather than adding to cart is an act of rebellion against a consumer culture that wants to rush us through the checkout process before we have time to think – and it's a major step towards mindful spending.

Beyond 'stuff': navigating a complicated relationship with consumption

As our awareness of the climate crisis grows, and the problems with mass production of fashion and consumables become more and more visible to us, our relationship with buying things grows ever more complex. Seeing the impact that our purchases are having on the planet imbibes our emotional spending complexes with an added layer of shame and guilt, but does it really act as a deterrent for most of us? After all, if being aware of the damaging implications of our actions was all it took to create better habits, financial wellbeing probably wouldn't be such an elusive concept in the first place. Our relationship with consumption is, in many ways, completely broken, and a necessary part of learning to spend mindfully is re-evaluating how we engage and the part that we play. Activist, consultant and author of *Consumed*,[1] Aja Barber, has some thoughts on the main factors that make our relationship with consumption so toxic:

'Not only is this cycle damaging to ourselves and our wallets, but it's also damaging to the planet. Our way of mass-producing items (whether it be clothing or other material possessions) for rapid consumption is ruining the planet and filling up landfills. The root of the consumption problem is discontent, and I think social media has played a huge part in that, fuelling our need for more, more, more every time we sign on to Instagram or elsewhere. We don't talk about mindfulness enough in our society and figuring out what is "enough", whether it's clothing or other items or even money. Once we really figure out what it is that we need, what we find is that many of us can actually live on . . . less.'

That hedonic treadmill again. When we see similar themes crop up in each step of the journey towards financial wellbeing, I like to think that it demonstrates the strength of this approach, and how each of the steps, even as they follow on from one another, are interlinked and contributing to a bigger picture of financial health and general wellbeing. Whichever way you cut the cake, the layers are the same, and the work that Aja does spans far wider than money or personal wellbeing – it helps us to see how our actions impact society and the planet that is our only home too.

I asked Aja whether there was a penny-drop moment for her, and whether there were any pointers she could share for anyone else looking to re-evaluate their relationship with consumerism.

'One year I added up my receipts from one fast fashion store that I used to frequent. I was HORRIFIED by the amount I was spending,' she said. 'Coupled with the knowledge I was beginning to grasp about garment worker treatment and environmental damage, I knew then and there that I had to make a change. None of these purchases were "harmless" and as I grasped the impact, I began to feel quite frustrated that I hadn't seen it sooner. Of course, it's always an ongoing process for me. It's not a clean break at all because consumerism is really a pillar in a lot of societies. I tend to really investigate my purchases now. But I will say once I stopped consuming clothing like water, I felt like my mind was clearer and I found that I was actually saving money (which is slightly embarrassing to acknowledge).

'I also recommend moving overseas,' she laughed. 'Having to pare down my possessions by 75% made me vow that I would never amass that number of items again in my adult life. Just moving in general is a good exercise in looking at your materialism sideways. There's always a moment when I'm moving where I want to dump the contents of my house in the local trash dumpster. Which tells you everything about what I need. Now every time I'm in a store and feel the temptation to buy something I may not absolutely need, I always ask myself, "but would I want to move this?" If the answer is "no", it stays in the store.'

Aja's ideas about having certain commitment and lifespan criteria for purchases that you might make are critical to mindful spending. Committing to buying less doesn't necessarily mean suddenly becoming a minimalist – it's more about really acknowledging that the things you buy are coming to live with you for the foreseeable future. Decades of viewing everything as disposable, from footwear to homeware, has made us forget that we're meant to buy things for the long haul – things that we actually like and want to use, rather than things we've seen looking cute on an influencer. When we spoke, Aja also had some brilliant suggestions for how we can start to spend more intuitively and in line with our own values, rather than according to fleeting whims and feelings of comparison.

'The type of rapid consumption we do in the US and UK is often habitual and it's important to recognize that first and foremost. But it doesn't help that you've got politicians telling you to go out and spend to "help" the economy, like it's our job to restore something so easily broken,' she warned. 'The first thing I always tell people is please stop buying so much. I'm not going to sit here from a perch of judgement because I used to be quite the fast fashion consumer, but the minute I started to question it, the process of constantly buying was immediately less appealing to me. The more time I took away from the idea that I needed a new clothing item monthly, the more I started to question what I had been doing all along. I suggest to people that they take a break from the places they're tempted to spend at and replace those visits with other activities. Volunteering for example. Visiting art museums. I also suggest recognizing what pushes you to spend. Do you buy when you feel sad? When you need a burst of confidence? When you're bored? Investigate those feelings. Lastly, and this is the most important tip of all, unsubscribe and unfollow the places that get the bulk of your money so much that you feel hostage to them . . . break up with them immediately. If you can't live without, you can always go back. But having a soft break up might often turn into a hard one.'

As someone I often look to for guidance and insights into how to navigate consumerism, I found it encouraging that so much of what Aja had to say about how we can be kinder to ourselves and the planet were aligned with the pathways and values that we explore throughout this book, and how the wider ripple effects of our personal journeys towards financial wellbeing could create a social and environmental impact too. Sometimes it helps, when we're not feeling inclined to be led by our finances on these decisions, to have other reasons to challenge hedonic adaption and learn to live better, with less.

Easing spending anxiety

Much of the focus of the spending discourse tends to focus around the habit of spending *too much*, but there are a lot of people out there who struggle to bring themselves to spend anything at all, or experience terrible anxiety after parting with any amount of cash. In some ways, it's understandable that we focus on those who are haemorrhaging cash at an alarming rate, because this is the practice that poses the most immediate and direct threat to financial health; quite literally, the money is leaving the building, and we need to try to stop it, because it's difficult to have a good relationship with money that's no longer in your possession. Even in this book, a lot of time is given to helping you to understand why you might struggle to curb spending that's tied to emotions rather than conscious, logical decision-making, but spending too much or too freely is not the only way in which it's possible for your spending habits to influence your financial wellbeing.

For most of my adult life, this was not a problem for me – I very much leaned towards the overspending end of the spectrum, even when money was very tight. I gained some insight, though, after I finished paying off my debt and was starting to build some savings. I was even earning more than I had done previously, and had a lot more income at my disposal, but I would freeze before buying things, even when they were things that I or my family needed. Shortly after *Real Life Money* was published, the years-old, barely functioning laptop that I wrote it on started to overheat after about thirty minutes of use. I had promised myself that, when it stopped working, I'd buy myself something decent – a MacBook, which I've always preferred, despite the cries of 'It's a waste unless you use all the design features' – and now was the moment. I had the cash, it was deductible as a business expense, and I was able to get a discount. But I couldn't do it. I dithered and dithered, only going through with the purchase when I grew so frustrated by my computer that I almost threw it out of the window. I found it very difficult, emotionally, to part with that cash, and the MacBook, when it arrived, felt *illicit*. I didn't feel deserving of it, and I dwelled on what else that cash could have paid for more than was healthy.

Otegha Uwagba describes this anxiety in far more detail and with far deeper context in her memoir, *We Need to Talk About Money*.[2] Her painful awareness of the fact that her family did not have enough money while she was a child led her to cling to money as an adult, and she describes how her relationship with money and sense of financial wellbeing has improved as she has allowed herself to let go a little. A much-needed reminder that, at its extreme, being 'good with money' – i.e. saving every penny and worrying over every purchase – does not necessarily equate to an easy or harmonious relationship with your finances. If you are not able to enjoy the money that you work so hard for, whether that enjoyment comes from spending, saving or a bit of both, then there may be something amiss, and tackling that could help you to squeeze a little bit more pleasure out of life, and fret a little bit less.

Perhaps unsurprisingly, much of the advice around spending anxiety that's already out in the mainstream is aimed at people who have a pressing reason to be anxious about money – if it's very tight, or there are debts to be settled etc. But, as with any type of anxiety, the threat doesn't have to be real or true in order to have a huge hold over you, so when I was trying to work out how to navigate this new feeling of struggling to let go of money, I looked to general anxiety advice for guidance. Here are a few ways that you could start to soothe that analysis paralysis, and quieten the anxiety that follows a purchase:

- Write down your reasons for making the purchase. Seeing them in black and white can really help a decision to feel properly considered – even if the reason is just 'I've wanted this for a while, and I can afford it'.
- Talk to someone that you trust. Often, hearing yourself explain the reasons why you feel anxious can help you to settle.

- Remind yourself, out loud if necessary, that the threat to your financial security and safety that you're imagining *isn't real*.
- Take some deep, relaxing breaths, or try repeating the self-trust meditation from Step One.
- If you're worrying about a purchase that you've already made, try distracting yourself with an activity that doesn't leave any room for anxious thoughts – something that gets you into a state of flow.
- Similarly, if you are sitting at home or in front of a screen dwelling on having spent money, try to get out of the house and into some green space.

The chances are that a lot of this misplaced anxiety around spending will be eased as you start to unpack your financial baggage, and come to terms with your relationship with money in the past, whether the factors leading to this anxiety are a product of your childhood or upbringing, or a product of decisions that you have made and rectified in the past – whether it is something that you inherited, or a case of 'once bitten, twice shy'. Hopefully, having worked through Step One, you will have started to process your past relationship with money and the factors influencing it, and now feel ready to implement some changes in the way that you think about and engage with money, which should, in turn, help to ease this anxiety and make you feel more confident in your decisions – so that you can enjoy the money that you earn.

Spending with intention and attention

This is really the definition of mindful spending – ensuring that you are giving all of your transactions your full attention, and that you are spending because you really want or need to. It sounds incredibly simple but, as you will know from experience, requires discipline and strength. As we've repeatedly seen, the choices that contribute positively to our financial wellbeing often do not lie on the path of least resistance; they are challenging, and they force us to confront things that aren't always comfortable. In order to start putting our mindful spending theory into practice, we need to apply these principles of intention and attention to all of our purchases going forward, giving ourselves the time and space that we need to make informed choices where possible.

It is up to you to decide the parameters of your own decision-making process when it comes to parting with your money – you need to be able to trust yourself to make the right choice for you as part of your ongoing financial wellbeing practice. Here are a few prompts and enquiries that you can make of yourself, though, before you head to the checkout or press the 'pay now' button.

You don't need to make all of your purchasing decisions based purely on affordability, by which I mean that just because you can afford to buy something, doesn't mean that you have to. It's a question of priorities, and whether you would rather invest the money in this product, or in something else.

- How do you imagine it will feel to own this product? How do you imagine feeling when you wear, admire or sit on it?
- Are you distracted, or are you fully focussed on this decision?
- Do you actually want (or genuinely like) this product, or do you want to buy it because you hope that it will somehow change *you* or the way that you feel about yourself?
- Are you going to use and enjoy it right away? If not, why not wait a while?
- Is this purchase going to contribute to, or damage your wellbeing in the long term?
- Is this purchase in your best interests, or are you making it to please or impress someone else?

Getting into the habit of gently probing yourself before you make spending decisions will help you to be present and conscious in the moment, and if you repeat some or all of these questions to yourself as you ponder your purchases, eventually these criteria will become second nature, and mindful spending will become more automatic. Until then, follow your methods for habit-building, and you'll be fine.

Here are a few ways to create a better, easier environment for your mindful spending habits to thrive:

Safeguards against impulse spending:

- Unsubscribe from marketing emails and opt out of push notifications
- Delete shopping apps
- Remove your credit and debit card details from your device's autofill function
- Close 'buy now, pay later' accounts
- Sleep on non-essential purchase decisions
- Calculate how long it would take you to earn the money that you're about to spend
- Enlist a spending accountability buddy
- Have a phone curfew and use that time for self-care
- Keep a running list of things that you like, want or need

Saving for enjoyment

We've discussed the importance of saving rituals, and we'll go into more detail about the various ways in which you can save and invest for a bright financial future a little later on. This section, though, is about creating a fund of completely disposable money. Two of the big elements in a dysfunctional relationship with spending are guilt and anxiety. Both of these feelings can contribute to either a terrible fear of spending or a compulsion to overspend, or both. How we respond to those feelings of guilt and anxiety is individual to each of us, but our natural response is often something that will be in direct conflict with financial wellbeing.

One of the ways that we can try to combat this is by creating a pot of money that is exempt from any kind of over-analysis or 'sensible' spending. Having a pool that you can dip into without buyer's remorse or a dent in your everyday budget can help you to regulate your feelings around spending and, therefore, your spending behaviour itself. It is a way to break the emotional spending cycle without inadvertently making overspending more inevitable – let me explain:

When we set spending on non-essentials up as the big bad behaviour that we want to avoid, as the antithesis of being 'good with money', we risk creating a go-to behaviour for every time that we feel we've fallen off the wagon of perfect financial behaviour. The more we see spending as a vice, the more we might tend to use it as a crutch, because we make it both more enticing and more punishable when we tell ourselves that it's entirely forbidden. Some people that I've spoken to even go as far as describing this way of spending as self-harm – a way of punishing yourself for any perceived financial misdeeds.

This is where giving yourself an amount of money that you can spend without guilt comes in handy, because it allows you to give yourself permission to spend on 'treats' and other non-essentials that you might otherwise baulk at. This in turn lessens, and eventually eliminates, the guilt and shame that often perpetuate this cycle. It's hard at first: you have to set boundaries with yourself and your thoughts in order to avoid the automatic wonderings about whether there was something more worthy that you should have spent the money on, but you can train yourself to treat this money differently, and it can make a real difference in the pursuit of that sense of money neutrality, i.e. being able to sever the connection between your finances and your self-worth and treat money as a tool.

This idea of a bank of savings just for enjoyment, or a 'slush fund' as he called it, was suggested to me in a call with Dr Ash Ranpura, a neuroscientist that I was working with on a campaign. He suggested that any unexpected, trivial or gifted amounts of money were used to fund this pot – Christmas or birthday money, say, or cashback on purchases or refunds for things like late trains. We all know how quickly these small amounts of money disappear in the wilds of our current accounts, but in diverting them to a slush fund, we give them a purpose and ourselves a way of spending money on ourselves without feeling guilty.

True self-care is not for sale

How did we allow looking after ourselves to become so commodified? At what point did the act of trying to feel okay, trying to feel *well*, go up for sale? These are questions that I ask myself on a regular basis, a provocation that I use to refocus my brain when it starts to look for commercial self-care solutions. Having spent my teenage years as a disciple of advertising slogans telling me that I deserved a certain product, that I was 'worth it', that only XYZ would make me feel whole and good, I struggle not to reach for fast fashion or beauty products as a quick-fix solution to a bad mood – and I know that I'm not alone in this. It can be really difficult to tell what we're genuinely doing for ourselves, to enjoy or relax us, and what we're spending in an attempt to cancel out the various stresses that come along with modern life. As lovely as an aroma-therapy massage is, it's not an antidote to an overwhelming mental load. It's a bit like trying to put out a fire with a thimble-ful of water – and it doesn't make any difference if the water is lavender-scented.

What's more, there is a weird tendency in the press and on social media to conflate self-care and personal grooming, the latter of which is really just a single element of looking after yourself. Actual self-care is complex, and sometimes it's *hard*. It doesn't just mean buying yourself whatever you want, all the time, or doing whatever you feel like at any given moment. It often means holding yourself accountable and practising self-discipline. Sometimes self-care is giving yourself a break, but sometimes it's doing the hard thing, or the annoying little thing that's been lingering on your to-do list for months.

Sometimes the hardest part of looking after ourselves can be working out what we do actually need, especially if we've been conditioned to reach for commercial solutions to our tiredness and discontent. I spoke to psychologist and author Suzy Reading, whose books on self-care contain some of the most nourishing, insightful advice I've ever read on this topic.

Aside from the fact that conversation with Suzy feels, in itself, like self-care of the highest order, her insights come from a place of truly understanding what it means to be human and to be flawed, and to still deserve to feel cared for. She encourages the people she reaches through her books and social media, as well as her practice as a psychologist, to reframe the way that they think of self-care, rejecting the way that our culture often conflates looking after yourself with buying things for yourself.

'Self-care has become commodified for sure,' she says. 'We need to move away from identifying self-care with products, or even practices. It needn't be either of those things, we could actually take a look at self-care as a skill set. These are things that you don't have to spend any money on to integrate into your life, but they do literally change the lens through which you see life unfolding.'

Suzy also has a refreshing take on mindfulness, with an awareness that many of us may have already heard of it, or even attempted to engage with it in a superficial or half-hearted way, and subsequently dismissed it. Again, it is a simple concept which has been commodified, and it's now difficult to picture mindfulness without thinking about colouring books and such. But, as with most of these things, it's about looking at that concept and asking yourself how we can apply it to our own lives in a way that makes sense to us, and in a way that's going to enhance our experience of life, rather than detract from it. It's the same with nutrition, exercise and – you guessed it –

money. We do not always have to follow someone else's interpretation of what it means to look after ourselves.

Suzy says 'I think we're all pretty well versed in mindfulness, but how do we actually make mindfulness feel juicy? Well, it's looking at specific applications of mindfulness. I think all of the skills are sort of a better use mindfulness. Maybe it's tapping into curiosity, maybe it's seeking a sense of wonder. It could be savouring where you suck the life out of pleasurable experiences, or you reminisce, or you anticipate future joys, it's bearing witness to connection. And, you know, that sense of shared humanity is in appreciation, and gratitude and kindness and compassion. So, I think if we can see at least part of our self-care as these things, none of those things cost a penny. When you become skilled at those things, that's when you start to feel less pushed around by life.'

And who doesn't want to feel that way? For many of us, that's what we're seeking when we cast about ourselves for self-care – the feeling of being less pushed around by life, of claiming something for ourselves, on our own terms.

In order to discover what it really means to properly look after ourselves, we need to take things right back to the Maslow hierarchy, and work our way up from the base level to the top, making sure that we are satisfying our own individual basic needs before we go in search of more superficial self-care solutions. Then we'll be able to value those experiences that we do decide to invest our hard-earned cash in. Think about it – there is no point paying for a massage when what you actually need is a nap, a glass of water, a favourite book and some nutritious vegetables – but if your mind and body are already feeling well-rested, well-nourished and well-hydrated, a massage can be a truly valuable experience.

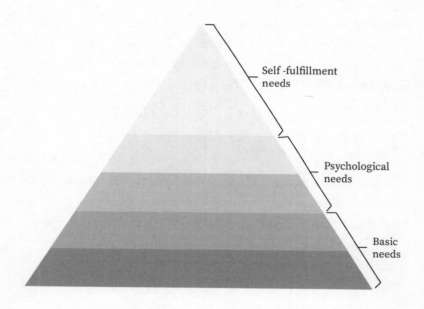

As we each have difference circumstances, means and priorities, there is scope here for us to each create our own pyramid of needs based on our own lives, which can help us to identify any gaps lower down that can't be solved with a spa day. For a new (or even not-so-new) mum, there might be a huge gap where sleep should be, which is leading to a compulsion to buy things as compensation, while someone working long hours might spend as a way to make up for a lack of leisure time, or for missing out on good company and rest. Someone feeling disconnected from friends and family, especially following the long months of isolation and loneliness that kicked off the 2020s, might spend as a way to assuage or quieten those feelings. If we can find a way to visualize this, and to tap into those gaps in our true self-care that we all know are there, deep down, then we should be able to start taking care of our wellbeing in a more comprehensive and authentic way, and remove the need for expensive sticking plasters and distractions.

Exercise: Your hierarchy

Can you start now? Consider Maslow's hierarchy and sketch out your own, thinking about what you need to feel whole and well. Look at the places where there are gaps and think about the role that those gaps play in your relationship with money. Is there something making you feel unsafe, that makes you afraid to spend a single penny, or obsessed with checking your bank balance? Is there something that you perceive to be missing elsewhere that you feel the need to compensate for with overspending – such as home-ownership or employment? Refer to the different tiers in Maslow's model, and really see if you can create a meaningful reference for understanding your spending behaviour.

Concluding thoughts for Step Four

Addressing issues with spending – whether you struggle to part with cash even for things that you really want or need, or you use spending as a crutch when things are difficult, or you flit anxiously between the two – can take time and practice. But as so much of our relationship with money revolves around our spending and saving practices, it's vital that we learn to feel comfortable and in control of these behaviours. Using the insights and techniques in this step, I hope that you can now recognize the unhealthy elements of your spending behaviour, and start to heal them. Being able to do this will help you to work towards that feeling of calm control over your money – you'll never be left wondering where all of your cash has gone a few days before pay day, and feelings of buyer's remorse and spending anxiety should be few and far between.

Control over the flow of cash out of your bank account will enable you to tell that voice – the voice of self-doubt, the one that wants you to define yourself as 'bad with money' for ever more – to kindly shut up, and it will help you to lay those financial demons and feelings of guilt to rest, finally. It will also, crucially, give you a brilliant foundation on which to make plans for your financial future, which is what we'll be discussing in Step Five. I'll meet you there.

Actions for Step Four

- ❏ Identify your triggers for emotional spending by looking at past spending behaviour.
- ❏ Reframe the way that you see desirable objects – do you need to possess them to appreciate them?
- ❏ Reconsider your relationship with consumerism, and focus on other motivations for reducing how much you consume.
- ❏ Protect yourself by taking practical steps to reduce your exposure to tempting marketing, such as unfollowing brands and influencers, and unsubscribing from emails.
- ❏ Commit to taking at least twenty-four hours to consider new purchases.
- ❏ Make sure that you fulfil your basic needs before looking for something new to buy.

Step Five

Planning and preparing for the future

The final step in our journey towards financial wellbeing was a late addition – when I first started trying to pull together some kind of framework for the kinds of conversations that I wanted to have about finding peace in our relationships with money, there were just four steps, or pillars. But I had a nagging feeling that something was missing, and I realized that, for most of us, feeling financially secure in the present isn't quite enough to allow a full sense of financial wellbeing to flourish. I realized that I had covered dealing with the financial past, and being mindful and present in the moment, but neglected to talk about planning ahead, even as I was making my own plans for a financial future beyond debt and living month-to month. If the events of the early 2020s so far have taught us anything, it's that your whole life – including your financial prospects – can change very quickly indeed, due to factors that are completely out of your control, and this has made a lot of people painfully aware of how financially precarious they are.

Planning for the future is not only essential for your motivation and drive, but it's also really important for those key elements of financial wellbeing that we discussed earlier in the book: security and freedom. It doesn't really matter whether you're the kind of person who likes to plan things to the letter, or whether you like to go with the flow, looking after your financial future and ensuring that your resources are fairly distributed between your present self and your future self will only ever improve your relationship with money. It will help you to navigate bumps in the road, and encourage you to feel positive about money, at least for the most part. The degree of detail to which you plan for your financial future is entirely up to you, of course, but taking steps to grow something for the life that you want to lead will only ever be a positive thing.

When I was struggling with my relationship with money, my ideas about the future of my financial situation were not rooted in reality at all – pretty much every idea I had about the life I'd like to live was dependent on some kind of extreme change in fortune, rather than on me sowing the seeds of a prosperous future in the present and watching them grow. Then, when I started to work on my financial wellbeing and take steps to repay the money that I owed, for a long time I felt like I was too busy filling in holes and correcting mistakes from the past to even think about the future. When I finally began to see the light at the end of that tunnel, and when much of the other work I was doing on my financial wellbeing was underway and starting to produce results – namely, the themes we have covered in the previous four steps – I began to think about planning ahead, and it really cemented the changes that I had begun to see in my feelings towards money, and also how I felt about myself. I found that I was no longer defining myself as someone who would never get on the property ladder, or never have savings, because I was entering a world where those things were looking more and more possible.

So, this final step is your opportunity to put some faith in your present self, and look out for your future self too. I really think that, once you've worked through the observations and exercises that follow, you'll start to feel a growing sense of wellbeing and positivity about your future, financial and otherwise.

Designing your lifestyle and setting goals

When I spoke to Anna Codrea-Rado about work and earning, and the impact of those factors on our self-worth, she mentioned the importance of 'lifestyle design', and the fact that we're neither taught how to manage our expectations of the kind of lifestyle we want, or to match our career and earning potential to the future that we see for ourselves. She is, of course, right. None of us are taught this kind of valuable information at school or even university, and if your parents don't teach you about the value of money and what living a certain lifestyle actually costs – or if, not uncommonly, they have their own hang-ups and issues around money – it can be really difficulty to align your income with your lifestyle. The generational difference in how much you need to earn to afford a certain lifestyle or financial comfort and security is also quite huge, meaning that aiming for the same lifestyle trajectory as your parents, even while working in a similar job and having similar spending habits to them, might just be completely impossible.

Taking a better-late-than-never approach to this, now is as good a time as any to start thinking about your lifestyle, what you want for your future, and how well that matches up to your income or earning potential. This potentially opens up lots of different questions, because most of us commit to, and work hard at, a particular career from our early to mid-twenties onwards, if not earlier, and making a change can feel huge and daunting. But it's better to look at the reality of what your career will afford you, because if your career path and your lifestyle aspirations are wildly out of sync, it can create a perfect storm of resentment and frustration, or push you to make ill-advised credit decisions as you struggle to afford the lifestyle that you want on the salary that you've got. But it doesn't have to be that way. Focusing on creating a lifestyle that will make you happy above and beyond material wealth and the numbers on your bank statement is a much better approach than focussing on monetary amounts, and identifying the best places to use your resources in order to squeeze maximum happiness and fulfilment out of them is at the core of lifestyle design. Think about how you want to live, look at what you've got, and its potential to grow, and figure out the best way to make those things fit together.

> **Exercise: Aligning your resources and your lifestyle aspirations**
>
> Take a moment – or perhaps slightly longer than a moment – to think about this. Are your career and lifestyle goals aligned, and are they moving at a similar pace if so? If not, are there some adjustments to either your circumstances (where possible), or your expectations about your time-lines or aspirations that you need to make? It may well be that, in moving through the previous steps of this process, you've re-evaluated some of your lifestyle aims and desires anyway, but now is a really good time to reflect and meditate on this a little, journaling it out if this is helpful.

An extra habit: setting and reviewing financial goals

Once you've sought to create some balance between the lifestyle that you want, and the lifestyle that your income will afford you, you should be in a good place to look at setting some financial goals. Goal setting is another common practice in both wellbeing and personal finance discourse, but it's important, when the goal is to focus on our financial well-being, to make sure that both are applied, and that our wellbeing goals and our financial goals align and complement one another.

The five habits that we explored in Step Three will, if established and adhered to, provide us with a really solid basis for financial wellbeing. They will enable us to feel calm and in control of our finances, in the present, and shift our mindset towards a more positive engagement with our money. They should also enable us to avoid the hedonic treadmill and feel more content, less vulnerable to comparing ourselves in a negative light and more open to feelings of gratitude. But we still need something to keep us looking forward, and to help us to plan for our financial future. The habit that we need to look at here is setting and reviewing goals that will keep us motivated and encourage progress, without daunting or overwhelming us, and making us feel like we want to give up.

There is a fine art to setting effective goals in any area of your life, but things can get even more complex when setting financial goals. If you pin all of your happiness on a particular figure or milestone, it can be incredibly frustrating when you feel as if you're not getting there fast enough. This can lead to taking on too much and then burning out, cutting corners and losing sight of why you actually want to achieve that goal in the first place. For example, if you'd like to earn/save/invest a certain amount in order to be able to afford to work part-time and spend more time with your loved ones, but the pursuit of that goal is taking you away from them in the intervening months and years, this is counterproductive. Or if you have a certain business goal in mind – let's say a six-figure turnover – but the pursuit of that goal is damaging your relationship with clients and customers and decreasing the lifespan or value of your business long term, this is also not a great idea. So, it's worth bearing in mind that, particularly with money, more and sooner is not always better, and setting your goals around sustainable progress is probably the right way to go.

The first thing to look at, when you start to consider your financial goals, is your inspiration. In pinning specific goals to a bigger-picture idea of what you want your future to look like, you give your goals texture, context and meaning. This, in turn, is motivating – if you can imagine how hitting a particular goal will improve your experience of life, whether that's affording you a nicer lifestyle, giving you more time or adding to your freedom, you will be more likely to actually follow through with them.

The second step is to look at your current situation, always acknowledging the positives, of course, and examine the gap between where your finances are, and where you'd like them to be. The size of that gap will influence how ambitious your goals need to be, and will also, to some extent, dictate the timescale for creating your goals. Make sure that, in doing this, you don't start to resent your current situation – remember that this is all a journey, and that the ability to set goals and look forward with positivity is, in itself, a huge achievement.

Exercise: Setting some goals

With that in mind, I'd like you to carefully consider up to three goals that you'd like to start working on now – one short term, one long term and perhaps one medium term. Write them down. You might also like to share these with a friend or your accountability buddy as a declaration of your faith in your ability to achieve them, and a way to ensure that you are answerable for taking actions that will guide you towards them.

Set a reminder or calendar entry to make sure that you check in on your goals at regular intervals, to make sure that you're making progress and moving towards them, but also to make sure that your goals are still right for your circumstances. Once a month, or even every three months is a good rule of thumb – checking them too frequently will only frustrate you and narrow your vision.

Aligning your financial plans with your personal values

An often-overlooked element of financial wellbeing is that most of us are very aware of the fact that our money has a life beyond its brief time within our possession, and that where we direct it actually matters. Some of the spending guilt that sits within us may well come from a place of regretting who we have given our money to, as well as what we received for it in return, in the form of goods or services. There is a growing reluctance, among many of us, to buy from huge companies with billionaire owners and underpaid workers, and more awareness of our ability to vote for the world that we want via the money that we spend, bank and invest. Initiatives such as Black Pound Day and local or independent spending drives have educated us in what it means to contribute to the economies that we want to see thriving, as well as withholding our cash from those companies that would use it to pay huge dividends to shareholders rather than pay their staff a living wage.

Again, this type of thinking can be a welcome reframe when it comes to our purchasing, banking and investing decisions in the present, but it can also help us to plan for our own financial future and enrich our own financial wellbeing by seeing what happens when we work to redistribute wealth in the way that we use our money. Ethical money collective Good Money Week have identified the following things that you can do to direct your money towards more ethical channels, supporting causes such as the environment, human rights and equality, as you also work on your own financial future:[1]

- Demand a clean and green pension – find out more about your pension provider, and ask to switch funds or even providers if your pension is being invested in causes with which you don't feel morally comfortable.
- Move your savings – even money in a simple savings account will give your chosen bank capital to invest and

make loans. Saving your money with an ethical bank will ensure that your savings are supporting kinder, greener investments and more ethical lending practices.

- Invest local – you can put your money into green local council schemes, such as solar farms, with a low-risk financial return.
- Speak to a financial advisor who specializes in green and ethical options – you can find a list at www.ethicalinvestment. org.uk/.

A great place to find out more about aligning your money goals and actions with your personal values is www. ethicalconsumer.org/, where there's loads of information and guides to which banks and accounts to try.

Take some time to think about the kind of world that you want to live in, and research ways to use your purchasing and investing power to play your part. This could mean investing in companies that are combatting climate change, which is becoming easier and more accessible thanks to new technologies and a boom in robo-investor start-ups, or simply choosing to make more of your purchases from small and ethical businesses. Especially if your relationship with money is affected by beliefs about money being evil, or a discomfort with the role that money often plays in the flaws and injustices in our society, using your money for good as you create your financial future might help you to rewire your feelings towards it, without leaving you struggling financially yourself.

Having a safety net and something to grow

Circling back once again to those pillars of financial wellbeing, freedom and security, part of building a positive financial future means putting aside what you can for when the unexpected happens, and growing your money so that you can eventually start to prioritize other things.

Creating a fund to be used in case of emergencies or unexpected turns of events has taken on a new significance in this post-pandemic era because, whether our work and income have been affected or not, we have all seen just how suddenly and completely things can change. The myriad ways in which we have no control over certain things have been demonstrated to us in a fairly violent fashion, as we saw everything about our lives turn into something new and alien. We adapted to the new circumstances, and life went on for most of us, but I think that the feeling of absolute powerlessness in the face of a force much bigger than us as individuals will stay with us all for a long time. With this in mind, at least part of our financial wellbeing is necessarily dependent on having a cushion to fall back on in case we need it.

Different people have different views about what size of 'emergency fund' is advisable, so it's really up to you to decide what you feel comfortable with, and what you feel is achievable for you. You might like to aim for three months' worth of bills and expenses to begin with, which should cover you for a period of earning-loss between jobs, or you might prefer to aim for six or twelve months; it depends entirely on you and what will make you feel secure. It will take time to build your emergency fund, but setting aside a small portion of your income each month for this is a good use of your cash, because it's a way of protecting yourself from hardship and difficulty that could sabotage the positive steps that you've taken in your relationship with money to date. So, having an emergency fund gives you security, but it also lends you some freedom too. It gives you the freedom to say no, and to enforce boundaries that you might have previously worried would impact you financially. It might grant you the financial independence that you need to leave an abusive partner or a job that's destroying your mental health, and having the knowledge that you don't have to put up with bad behaviour or being hurt in order to keep paying the bills is incredibly liberating. Having some money saved puts a lot of decisions back into your hands, and allows you to put your safety, happiness and wellbeing first.

Once you have some emergency savings in place, it's time to start thinking about how you can grow your money in order to give you more options in the future – always, of course, in line with your own lifestyle goals and what's realistically possible within your means. The conversation around investing has changed a lot in recent years and, as interest rates on savings have plummeted and stagnated, investing your money has become one of the best ways to beat inflation and ensure that you don't actually end up losing money on your savings.

Of course, most pensions are also a form of investing – and an element of financial wellbeing that is often neglected, because we assume that it's something that we don't need to think about until 'later'. It's never really too early or too late to start thinking about investing in funds or your pension, but there are a few elements of your financial health that it's wise to have under wraps before you start to invest your money:

- Paying off problem or expensive debt
- Having that emergency fund saved
- Successfully living with your budget, and within your means
- Having some monthly funds – even as little as £10 – that you don't need and won't miss

Once you meet these criteria, it's a good idea to learn the basics of the stock market and research the different investing options available to you – and not on TikTok. In fact, it's a good idea to be cautious about any investing advice on social media, because there are some rogue ideas out there from unaccredited sources. The very last stumbling block anyone needs on their journey towards financial wellbeing is to lose money on risky investments. The right approach is usually slow and steady, with a wish to grow your money over a number of years, rather than seeing investing as a short-term money-making gambit. See the Further Reading section at the back of this book for a couple of good books to use as a starting point. There is now an absolute wealth of ethical investing options, including with most pensions, so if you'd rather avoid investing your money in things like fossil fuels, tobacco and arms, this might be a good option for you.

When you feel ready, you could look at making yourself a little saving and investment plan. This is something where a financial advisor or coach could be an option, and there are plenty of options for engaging someone to guide you through making financial decisions, including app-based coaching, but if you're feeling connected and confident with your finances, you could create something very simple yourself. Make sure that you look at things such as interest rates, accessibility and fees, to make sure that you're maximizing your return on the investment that you're making in your future.

Actively engaging with your finances to build something positive, rather than just trying to plug holes in your budget, is a really brilliant milestone in your financial wellbeing journey, and should be celebrated. I still remember the feeling of realizing that I had been sustainably saving for a whole year without having to withdraw what I'd set aside, and that I had some real savings for the first time in my adult life – and it felt like I'd won the lottery. But better than that, I knew that I'd been able to do it because I'd made real changes to my relationship with money, and that they were working. If you're feeling ready to focus on providing yourself with some freedom and security in the form of savings and investments, I hope that you feel proud too.

Saving for a home

What was once a fairly standard milestone in adult life for many has become a huge, sometimes seemingly unachievable, goal as property prices have rocketed over the last couple of decades. Depending on where you live, the amount that you need to save for a house deposit, and the amount you need to earn to meet banks' mortgage affordability criteria, is really daunting. I've spoken to many fellow millennials who have said that their saving motivation has been all but extinguished by the intimidating target of the tens of thousands of pounds required for a down-payment, so they choose to divert their funds towards more immediate and enjoyable ventures.

And yet housing security is one of the 'safety' needs in Maslow's hierarchy. For all of us, having a roof over our heads and a fixed address is absolutely paramount not only to our wellbeing but to our ability to function in society. A home to call your own, whether you rent or have a mortgage, is a very basic human need, and yet housing security for private tenants in the UK is sketchy at best. Writing for the *Guardian* about 'the looming mental health crisis for Generation Rent',[2] Rhiannon Lucy Cosslett outlined the many ways in which insecure housing can affect our mental wellbeing, from frequent moves to having to relocate and leave support networks behind. 'A lack of housing affordability isn't just a question of cash,' she writes, 'It has the potential to affect our sense of stability, our wellbeing and mental health, and our family planning. A home is so much more than a roof over your head.'

Shortly before the pandemic hit, a request for some maintenance on the floor of our rented home was met, to our shock,
with the announcement that our landlords had sought financial
advice and decided to sell the property. For many landlords,
unfortunately, the homes that they own are seen purely as a
financial investment, and disruption to tenants' lives is
collateral damage that is barely worth a second thought – of
course #notalllandlords etc. But lots of them. The experience
of trying to arrange a house move on the morning of the first,
terrifying nationwide lockdown is not one that will leave me
any time soon, and it made me determined to channel as
much of my energy as possible into creating a more secure
housing situation for myself, my husband and our two young
sons. We already had our next financial goal lined up before
we had even finished paying off our debt, but having overcome
such a huge hurdle already, and having worked through the
challenges that we've covered in the previous steps, it felt
more achievable, even if we were going to have to be patient
and work hard. I have found saving for a home to be quite
unique, both in terms of the actual logistics, and also in an
emotional sense too. Saving should always feel like a positive
act, but in saving for a house, I can almost visualize the building forming, brick by brick, every time we make another
transfer into our savings account.

If you are on the same journey with regard to home-ownership,
or hope to be at some point in the future, it's a really good
idea to start scoping out your options, and seeing if any

government schemes or tailor-made savings accounts might help you to get there a little bit quicker.

Schemes and accounts to help you save a house deposit

Lifetime ISA

Replacing the now-defunct Help to Buy ISA, opening a Lifetime ISA will enable you to buy a property up to £450,000 when you use it to save your deposit. The government will top up your savings by 25% up to £4,000 per year, making this a great option for saving up to that amount. For example, if you put in £4,000 over the course of a year, you'll get a £1,000 top up, bringing your total to £5,000. This can only be used for a house deposit, or towards pension savings.

Shared Ownership

If you're struggling to save the deposit or afford the mortgage on 100% of a home, you can buy a share of between 25 and 75% of the property and pay rent on the rest. You can then buy a larger share of the property if and when you can afford it.

Equity Loan

This also gives you the option to reduce the deposit that you need and the amount of money you need to borrow on your mortgage, by allowing you to borrow between 5% and 20% (40% in London) of the value of the property as a loan, which is interest free for the first five years and is repaid alongside your mortgage.

NB: all the above have pros and cons. For more information about any of these schemes, see www.gov. uk/affordable-home-ownership-schemes.

Fixed-term Savings

For a non-government-backed option, you can often get better rates on savings accounts that don't allow you to withdraw for a certain period – usually at least two years. As long as you can be pretty certain that you won't need the money in the meantime, this can be a smart choice: higher interest and it's locked away.

The key, really, with saving for an important, long-term financial goal is to be patient and determined, but not to let it take over every second of the intervening weeks, months and (potentially) years. Allow it to be a pot that you keep simmering on the back hob, knowing that, when it's finally ready, it will taste amazing. Ensure that you're checking in every now and again, and celebrate when you reach certain milestones, even if you're not quite at the end yet. Saving £5,000 or £10,000 is a huge achievement – it doesn't matter if you're not even halfway to the end goal yet. Celebrating these wins will give you a boost of positivity, and make you feel rewarded for your hard work – and saving *is* hard work!

Saving for retirement

Pensions or retirement savings, with their indecipherable jargon and lack of immediate usefulness, risk becoming an abstract, far-away concept that we ignore until it suddenly feels too late to do anything about and we're at panic station. It makes sense, after all – for Millennials and Gen-Zs, there are many other intimidating financial milestones to conquer before we feel we can start prioritizing a pension (see: saving for a house). And yet, that nagging sense that we should be putting something towards our retirement worries at the back of our minds, eroding our sense of financial security and well-being and stopping us from being able to imagine our future beyond our working years.

Of course, getting and subsequently paying off a mortgage will have a significant effect on your comfort in retirement, because accommodation, whether this is rent or mortgage payments, represents a huge proportion of most people's monthly outgoings. For this reason, lots of people find that housing security and getting on to the property ladder is priority number one, and a focus on pension savings comes later, which is completely sensible – all I want you to do is make sure that your pension is a consideration. Ensuring that you're enrolled in your workplace pension and contributing enough to get your employer contributions is a great idea, as soon as you start work.

I previously talked about investing as a way of growing wealth – but even if you've never heard of a stocks and shares ISA, you are most likely an investor already, through your pension. If you've ever paid into your company pension scheme, and it is now compulsory for your employer to do so, it's likely that your money is being invested to create your pension fund. It's important to know this, because when something is automatically deducted from your salary each month, you feel less connected with that money. It's like the tax that you pay as an employee, which you never see in your bank account. This is good, because you don't miss it or risk spending it, but it can also mean that you're missing an opportunity to really make the most of your pension, or even to ensure that your pension investments aren't in direct conflict with your personal beliefs and values, as I discussed earlier in this step. Taking an active interest in your pension and knowing how much you're contributing, as well as making sure that you are maximizing your employer contributions (if you're employed by a company), will really enhance those feelings of security and freedom that we've established as being vital for financial wellbeing.

If you're self-employed, the bad news is that there's nobody else to contribute to your pension – it's all you. But the good news is that it's super easy to get started with your pension using any number of fintech providers. A simple SIPP (Self-Invested Personal Pension) can take minutes to set up, and you can deposit regular amounts or lump sums according to what works best for you. If things get a little complex, it's also worth speaking to a financial advisor about setting things up in the right way.

It's also worth noting that, because of compounding – where the returns that you make on your pension investments are reinvested to make further returns (i.e. more money becomes even more money) – it's a brilliant idea to contribute to your pension from as early in your career as possible. Even a small amount, invested regularly from an early age and allowed to grow, will make a huge difference over the course of a few decades. However, if retirement seems to be approaching quicker than you'd like, and you're worried about your pension, it really is never too late to start.

Something that we really must cover, when it comes to pensions, is the gargantuan gender pension gap that exists. The average gap is 38%, rising to 57% in some areas of the UK,[3] and the gap is starker still for Black women and single mothers, among other under-pensioned groups.[4] People who fall into multiple under-pensioned categories may have a pension pot that is a mere fraction of the UK average, and an even smaller fraction of the average pension for men. There are a huge number of systemic failures that allow this to happen, from the gender and race pay gaps to the way that employer contributions and auto-enrolment are set up, but, if you're a woman, it's important to take action as early as possible to minimize this gap for your own future, if you possibly can. To give a common example, if you take a career break or reduce your working hours in order to fulfil a caring role – most typically after having a child – you might want to have a serious conversation about your working (or full-time working) partner contributing to your pension. It is a huge risk for women to rely on their partner's pension while caring their way into a precarious, under-pensioned position, and this risk undermines your future financial wellbeing. Of course, we all want to believe that our relationship will last for ever – and maybe it will – but similarly to having an emergency fund, knowing that your pension is going to be *enough* no matter what happens in your relationship is a much-needed comfort. There is no reason why a couple's decision to have a child should jeopardize the mother's (or, on rare occasions, the father's) pension only.

So, you see, pensions are really not just about having enough money to go to bingo. When you retire, you are still going to want to enjoy life as much as you do now, and to make the most of the extra time that you have after working for decades. Investing the time, effort and money needed to build up a good pension will be so worth your efforts, even if it's just a brief check every few months, an extra glance at your employment contract and an extra percentage point of your salary each time you get a pay rise. These small moves, made early enough, will help you to secure your financial wellbeing for the future, which will also help you to feel more confident and in control of your money in the present.

If you don't know where to get started with you pension, here are a few quick pointers:

- Track down any old pension pots from previous jobs. There are an estimated 1.6 million lost pension pots in the UK, totalling £19.4 billion[5] – don't let yours add to that figure! You can find old pensions using the tracker on gov.uk, but some pension providers have their own trackers, and will find and consolidate old pension pots for you.
- Add your pension provider(s) to that never-ending list of companies to update whenever you move house or change your name. It might take an extra half an hour at the time, but it'll save you time and worry later on.
- Ask your employer about your workplace pension. You could even ask them to bring your employee pension provider in to do a talk (this sounds like a snore-fest, I know, but a previous employer did this and it was genuinely fascinating).
- If you're self-employed, the statistics say that you probably don't have a pension. Time to change that – even if you're only paying in a small amount each month.
- Use a pension calculator (there are loads of different ones available) to work out what you need to save in order to comfortably retire.

This is absolutely not something that should be occupying your thoughts night and day, and checking your pension super-frequently or chopping and changing provider all the time is not going to contribute anything positive to your financial wellbeing. Just be aware, invest what you can, and make sure that you're taking advantage of any contributions from your employer, and you should be able to quieten that nagging voice in the back of your head telling you that you'll never be able to afford to retire.

Saving for your children

This could, of course, mean about a hundred different things. If you choose to have children, they are expensive in various and multifaceted ways, from restricting your income and requiring expensive childcare, to feeding and clothing them, and trying to ensure that they are set up for a stable financial future of their own. This is without even considering the hidden financial pressures that come from comparing yourself and what you're able to provide for your children with others around you – especially, of course, on social media. It's a lot of pressure.

If you're reading this before starting a family, but are planning to at some point in the future, one of the best ways that you can protect your financial wellbeing through parenthood is by setting up a saving pot for anything you might need to support you during maternity leave and the early, painfully expensive, years of childcare. I say this not because I think that your parenting ability or right to have children should ever de-pend on how financially stable or literate you are, but because I know the difference that this would have made to my own experience of early motherhood. Depending on when you imagine having children, you could even invest this money in order to achieve maximum growth, and sacrificing a small amount of money from your salary early on will make a big difference later.

If you already have children, that last paragraph may have given you flashbacks of struggling to manage financially through maternity pay and childcare, as it did me. But we all know that there are new costs for every stage, and starting to put money aside for the different things that your children will need can really take some of the stress out of family life. For example, in the same way that you might save throughout the year for car insurance, council tax or any other annual expense (many people call these sinking funds, and they work brilliantly for removing some of the bumps in your financial calendar), you could create saving pots for back to school, Christmas, birthdays and the summer holidays. Take a moment to calculate some estimated costs for these expensive events in the year, and then work out how much you would need to contribute to each, monthly. Then, see if there's space in your budget to work this in. Operating in this way, even just for some of these more costly times of the year, will help you to prevent cycles of debt and an over-reliance on credit cards, but will improve your overall financial confidence too. As with all of your saving habits, automating these small contributions just after you get paid will take most of the effort out of the process for you.

Beyond everyday family life and the costs involved with having and raising your children, the dearest wish of most people who've struggled in their relationship with money is to give their children the gift of financial security. There are two facets to this, the first of which is trying to pass on everything that you've learned throughout these five steps, giving your children access to a solid financial education and being open with them about money and the real role that its plays in our lives. The second is actually building up some savings that you can give to them to help them on their way – and one of the reasons why education and support are so important is that this will affect their ability to handle any money that you are able to pass on to them to start their adult lives.

Practically, one of the best ways to save for your children is with a junior ISA. This is a savings account set up in your child's or children's name, which they will be able to access when they turn eighteen – or a little later on, if you work with them to re-invest it until they're ready to spend it well! You can save up to £9,000 per year without paying tax on any interest or returns that you might gain. Junior ISAs, or JISAs, are available as cash accounts, where you will earn interest but probably not beat inflation, and stocks and shares accounts, where the money is invested and grown. If you start one of these accounts when your children are still young, and invest regularly, your money will have up to eighteen years to grow, maximizing that compounding effect that we discussed earlier and mitigating risk. With investing, your capital is always at risk, but markets grow and recover from dips over time. This is another thing that you might like to discuss with a financial advisor, but it's very easy to get started with a small amount each month.

Once I finished paying off my debt, creating financial security for my family was next on the priority list. This included saving hard for a house deposit, but I was also delighted to be able to open JISAs for both of my children, and put something small away for them each month. I check to see how they're doing every now and then, and it gives me a little burst of financial joy to know that I'm succeeding in that.

Making decisions about credit and debt

As someone whose whole career and platform was catalysed by a huge sum of personal debt and a mission to pay it off, it often surprises people that I don't take a more hard-line approach when it comes to people using credit or taking on debt. There's rarely space for much nuance in online conversations, and I've already discussed the fact that our cultural understanding of money is famously missing any nuance, so maybe it's no surprise that I'm assumed by some to be the face of the anti-debt movement. As with everything else in personal finance, your decision to use credit or take on debt is entirely personal to you. I sometimes worry that the discourse around encouraging people to take using credit seriously, and making sure that debt can be serviced without causing damage to mental health and wellbeing, risks wandering into the realms of judging consumers for their decisions rather than holding lenders accountable for their practice. What is deemed reasonable debt by some would be baulked at by others, in the same way that there will always be someone with different saving and spending priorities to you, and we need to be careful about acknowledging the line between equipping people with the information that they need and warning about predatory lenders, and further exacerbating the debt stigma that keeps so many people in a hole of guilt and shame. Largely, we are dealing with a trifecta of unfortunate truths about credit and debt: questionable ethics and motives on the part of some lenders, constant bombardment of credit opportunities everywhere from the sides of buses to the checkout on the ASOS website, and then the huge stigma around succumbing to any of these offers – especially if you find yourself in any kind of trouble. When you think about the impossible situation this leaves some people in, you begin to notice how broken it is that the system is essentially geared towards pressuring people to take on debt, then abandoning and chastising them if they struggle to manage it.

Having a healthy relationship with money, for many people, means being open to using credit and learning how to manage it well. The fear and stigma surrounding even small credit card balances can set any kind of non-mortgage debt up as a terrible, dirty secret, meaning that in situations where it's unavoidable, people enter a cycle of shame that can end up being very damaging to both finances and wellbeing over time. If you've had problem debt in the past, as I have, I've found that learning to use credit well can really help to heal some of that guilt and shame that might follow you even once the debt is paid off. The confidence that I feel in being able to use a credit card wisely and appropriately, pay off the balance each month and spread the cost of larger items cheaply, is a feeling that I coveted for such a long time when I was plagued by beliefs that I was 'bad with money'. One of the repeating themes in this book is the importance of learning to trust yourself to make the right decisions with money, and using credit can be a huge test of that – it's completely understandable if you'd rather avoid it altogether, but try not to be afraid of it.

So, how do we decide when credit could be a good option? Here are a few things to make sure you have in place before you borrow:

- You understand the terms of your agreement to borrow money, and any penalties or consequences if you can't pay.
- You've taken enough time to consider whether it's worth taking on this financial commitment.
- You can afford the repayments and have added them to your budget.
- You aren't just spreading or delaying the cost for the sake of it.
- There's a benefit to getting the product or service now, rather than waiting until you've saved up for it.

- You aren't over-committing yourself or making your budget too complicated to manage.

All of these considerations are designed to safeguard your financial wellbeing and to make sure that you aren't creating a stressful situation for yourself that will undermine the progress you've made, but I truly believe that we need to be more realistic and accepting about the role of credit in our society and daily lives, because this system whereby it is pushed and then stigmatized is not serving anybody's wellbeing or mental health. As with everything else, the key is to make sure that any use of credit is controlled and considered.

Accepting ebb and flow

A mistake that we often make in our expectations about what wellbeing means is that we think it should be constant. We assume that we will hit some kind of golden milestone, and everything will be perfectly balanced and harmonious from there on out – or at least I did for a long time. The truth is, though, that those moments of perfect balance actually happen very rarely, and nothing is ever still. Everything about our lives is in constant motion, and we can control the direction of some of that motion through our decisions and actions, but some aspects of our lives operate entirely independently from us. The sooner we are able to accept this, and to accept that we might still have to deal with unexpected turns of events or moments of financial stress and anxiety, the better equipped we will be to deal with those occasions when they arise. There might be times when we are earning more money and times when we are earning less, times when life is very expensive and times when we are able to live more economically. But once we create an environment of financial wellbeing and a strong, engaged relationship with money, these things become easier to navigate. A well-established system, whereby you aren't carrying excessive financial baggage, don't hang your self-worth on your financial situation, have rituals and habits to offer stability, feel in control of your spending and are mindful of the future – i.e. our five steps – will make you resilient to financial changes, large and small. When life throws you a financial curveball, you will have a safety net of beliefs, coping mechanisms and practical techniques to catch you.

Concluding thoughts for Step Five

Although much of our financial wellbeing is rooted in being present in the moment, creating habits to support us and feeling grateful for what we have, creating for ourselves a plan and a safety net for the future is also absolutely vital. We all know that things rarely go exactly to plan, but by having an outline for how you'd like to proceed with your finances, and the role that you'd like money to play in your future, you have a central point to pivot from when circumstances change.

There is certainly a balance to be struck between enjoying the money that you earn, and ensuring that you feel fulfilled and content in the present, and protecting the future version of yourself too. In planning for our financial future and taking steps in the present to protect and care for ourselves, we are doing our best to ensure that all of the needs in our hierarchy are met in the years to come. We are showing ourselves some care and consideration. Planning for your financial future is an act of self-care and self-respect, and it is one that you fully and richly deserve.

Actions for Step Five

- [ ] Consider the kind of lifestyle that you want for yourself, and make sure that there's not a big gap between your means and your aspirations.
- [ ] Set financial goals, and check back in on them as an additional habit. You could include this in your budgeting ritual, or treat it completely separately.
- [ ] Create a saving and/or investing plan for your money.
- [ ] Write a 'manifesto for credit' – a pledge to yourself to utilize credit and debt only in a way that serves you.
- [ ] Break big savings goals into manageable chunks.
- [ ] Learn to accept the ebb and flow of life and money, safe in the knowledge that you are doing everything you can to protect and nurture your financial wellbeing.

Finding financial wellbeing when . . .

One of the biggest problems with mainstream financial advice is that it makes assumptions about us that are often simply not accurate. Throughout the coronavirus pandemic, the degree to which individual circumstances can dictate our relationship with money became more difficult to ignore than ever before, and I started to wonder why mainstream finance platforms were so ignorant of this. I habitually read a lot of money content as part of my job – and there's a lot out there – but so many narratives were missing, and so much was oversimplified. The same old advice seemed to be churned out no matter the question or how it was framed. I started thinking about ways to change that, and, in March 2021, I started commissioning for a new content series that would share how overcoming adversity, or being marginalized by society, affected people's financial wellbeing, and hopefully help others by passing on anything these people had learned from navigating a hostile system. It was thrilling to be able to commission people to write about these topics, and the more perspectives I read, the better my understanding of money became.

If you'd like to deepen your understanding of why money is such a deeply emotional issue, and why some of us struggle more with it than others, then I'd love to humbly suggest that you read some of these essays at www.thefwforum.com, where you will also find guides and templates to support your own financial wellbeing journey. You might find something in there that makes you feel seen and supported, or something that opens your eyes and increases your empathy – and that's never a bad thing for your financial wellbeing.

Five steps for the future

I'm not sure that this process is something that you 'complete' – it's something ongoing. Some of the steps might bear revisiting or repeating, and your relationship with money may well be something that you re-evaluate and work on further, as things changed and evolve in your life. Keeping your home, health, work and interpersonal relationships in order is an ongoing practice, and so is managing your relationship with money, but you should now be able to do so from a place of better understanding, a higher sense of self-empathy and a clearer idea of what you actually want from your money. Wellbeing is not in stasis; it is in a constant state of flux. It is not something that happens to you, it is something that you *do*. Financial wellbeing is the environment in which you can thrive, rather than some final destination where the streets are made of gold.

The reason I started this book with unpacking your financial baggage is that I don't think many of us realize how heavy the load that we've been bearing is, and how much it influences our decisions and limits our outlook in the present. Processing and letting go of mistakes that we might have made, or things that have happened to us with regard to money, or at least making them lighter to bear, opens the doors to a world in which our financial past no longer dictates our financial future. Whether you're just starting to manage your finances independently, or you've already woven a rich tapestry of financial history, we all have hang-ups, regrets and reservations that pull us backwards, and laying them to rest will enable us to move forward.

Learning to live peacefully alongside your money, and to handle it with a sense of neutrality – to not allow it to define your self-worth or how capable you think you are – is a skill that must be honed over a period of time, and there will be moments where you might have to challenge your own thinking in order to make progress. Changing your viewpoint, learning to be grateful for what you have and how to look after yourself without relying on the solutions offered by capitalism and consumerism are just as key to your financial wellbeing as the practical steps that you can take towards financial security. If you don't feel capable or deserving of financial wellbeing, you will find it incredibly difficult to get there, so you have to make sure that you are fostering the self-worth and self-respect that you deserve, and enforcing the boundaries in your relationships that will make that possible.

Once we have laid the foundations for a good relationship with money in how we think about it and ourselves – and the relationship between the two – it becomes possible to create sustainable habits and rituals that will help us to engage with our finances in a positive and practical way. Each of these new habits is underpinned by the belief that we are equal to a task that many of us have found near impossible in the past: the task of feeling in control of our money, rather than it being in control of us. Through the small things that we build into our lives every day, and reframing tasks such as budgeting and organizing our bank accounts as something closer to self-care than life admin, we can create a framework of mutually supportive habits that will hold us and give us security, even when circumstances change.

For most of us, the amount that we can earn is finite, whether this is because we're in a job with a fixed salary or because we only have a certain amount of time and resource that we can exchange for money as freelancers and business owners. But what we can spend – the money that flows out of our accounts, is limited by nothing other than our credit limit and our self-discipline. This means that, in order to achieve financial wellbeing, we need to ensure that we're spending mindfully and in a controlled manner, at least most of the time. Our spending habits, and how we respond to marketing and consumer culture, are all heavily influenced by our emotions, and recognizing where our feelings and finances meet enables us to see the warning signs and feel more in control of our actions. Once you know the tricks that retailers use to get us to spend, it's easier to resist them, and once you identify the feelings that trigger unhealthy spending habits, it's easier to seek out other self-soothing techniques that don't rely on spending and won't end up costing you your wellbeing in the long run.

When your relationship with money is broken, it can feel impossible to look ahead, or to imagine that there is a future in which you are in control of your money and using it to make proactive, positive manoeuvres and decisions. In repairing it, you open up a world of possibilities, and creating a plan for your financial future will give you the sense of freedom and security that underpins a full sense of financial wellbeing. Looking at where your money is going and the future that it's helping to build, both in the wider world and in your own life, will help you to feel more connected to your finances, while knowing that you have a safety net and are working towards your goals will fulfil some of those vital needs in Maslow's hierarchy.

These five steps represent, in my opinion, the key building blocks of a healthy and happy relationship with money. They will give you a pathway for reaching your financial potential without sacrificing too many of your other resources or tricking you into thinking that your worth is dependent on your financial success. These steps take into account the whole being, rather than just the bank account, and many of the skills that you'll develop as you move through the stages are soft ones, but, in my lived and demonstrated experience, they work.

I hope that these five steps have helped you to learn something about your relationship with money, and equipped you with the tools that you need to make the changes that you need to. I hope that if you find yourself getting sucked back into old habits, letting your boundaries lapse or allowing your finances to dictate your self-worth, you will come back to them and carry on doing the work to support your financial wellbeing. Because if you do, I promise that the future is bright. It may not be easy, and it may not be instant, but in changing your relationship with money, you can change your whole life.

Notes

Introduction

1. Hilary Osborne, 'Financial inequality: the ethnicity gap in pay, wealth and property', *Guardian*, 20 June 2020, https://www.theguardian.com/money/2020/jun/20/financial-inequality-the-ethnicity-gap-in-pay-wealth-and-property
2. Abraham H. Maslow, *A Theory of Human Motivation* (1943).

1. Overcoming your financial baggage

1. https://www.alcoholics-anonymous.org.uk/about-aa/the-12-steps-of-aa
2. Glennon Doyle, *Untamed: Stop Pleasing, Start Living* (Vermillion, 2020).
3. https://www.womensaid.org.uk/information-support/what-is-domestic-abuse/financial-abuse/
4. In Good Company with Otegha Uwagba, 'Mona Chalbi:

Money Dysmorphia. Cultural Attitudes to Money',
https://www.podcasts.apple.com/gb/podcast/036-
mona-chalabi-money-dysmorphia-cultural-attitudes/
id1294215581?i=1000528835456

5. Mona Chalabi, 'Money dysmorphia: why I can't let
    myself have nice things', *Guardian*, 21 March 2019,
    https://www.theguardian.com/money/2019/mar/21/
    money-dysmorphia-cant-let-myself-have-nice-things

6. Agata Gasiorowska, 'The relationship between objective
    and subjective wealth is moderated by financial control
    and mediated by money anxiety', *Journal of Economic
    Psychology*, vol. 43, August 2014, pp. 64–74, https://
    www.sciencedirect.com/science/article/abs/pii/
    S0167487014000348

7. Nione Meakin, 'Do You Need Financial Therapy',
    Guardian, 5 January 2016, https://www.theguardian.
    com/money/2016/jan/05/do-you-need-financial-
    therapy

8. Jo Love, *Therapy is Magic: An Essential Guide to the Ups,
    Downs and Life-Changing Experiences of Talking Therapy*
    (Yellow Kite, 2021).

9. Clare Seal, 'Why Don't We Talk About Therapy
    Privilege?', *Grazia*, 7 May 2021, https://www.graziadaily.
    co.uk/life/real-life/therapy-privilege-mental-health-
    support-cost-prices-uk/

2. Separating your self-worth from your net worth

1. Anna Codrea-Rado, *You're the Business: How to Build a Successful Career When You Strike Out Alone* (Virgin Books, 2021).
2. Susannah Butter and Katie Strick, 'The Wing: how the 'feminist utopia' got it so wrong', *Evening Standard*, 7 July 2020, https://www.standard.co.uk/lifestyle/the-wing-rise-and-fall-a4491126.html
3. https://www.psychologytoday.com/gb/basics/hedonic-treadmill
4. Maslow, *A Theory of Human Motivation*, ibid.
5. Sonja Yubomirsky, Laura King, Ed Diener, 'The benefits of frequent positive affect: does happiness lead to success?', 2005, https://escholarship.org/uc/item/1k08m32k
6. https://www.instagram.com/nedratawwab/ (@nedratawwab)
7. Nedra Glover Tawwab, *Set Boundaries, Find Peace: A Guide to Reclaiming Yourself* (Piatkus, 2021).
8. ASA Ruling on DSG Retail Ltd t/a Currys PC World, 10 March 2021, https://www.asa.org.uk/rulings/dsg-retail-ltd-g20-1088321-dsg-retail-ltd.html
9. Doyle, *Untamed*, ibid.
10. Nedra Glover Tawwab, *Set Boundaries, Find Peace: A Guide to Reclaiming Yourself*, ibid.
11. Mo Gawdat, Solve for Happy: Engineer Your Path to Joy (Bluebird, 2019).

3. Creating money habits and rituals

1. James Clear, *Atomic Habits: An Easy & Proven Way to Build Good Habits & Break Bad Ones* (Random House Business, 2018).
2. https://www.nsandi-corporate.com/news-research/news/29-million-britons-worry-about-personal-finances-most-bury-their-heads-sand#
3. 'How it works – Cognitive behavioural therapy (CBT)', https://www.nhs.uk/mental-health/talking-therapies-medicine-treatments/talking-therapies-and-counselling/cognitive-behavioural-therapy-cbt/how-it-works/
4. Summer Allen, 'The Science of Gratitude', Greater Good Science Center, May 2018, https://www.ggsc.berkeley.edu/images/uploads/GGSC-JTF_White_Paper-Gratitude-FINAL.pdf
5. Robert. A. Emmons and Michael E. McCullough, 'Counting Blessings Versus Burdens: An Experimental Investigation of Gratitude and Subjective Well-Being in Daily Life', *Journal of Personality and Social Psychology* 2003, vol. 84, no. 2, pp. 377–389, https://www.emmons.faculty.ucdavis.edu/wp-content/uploads/sites/90/2015/08/2003_2-Emmons_McCullough_2003_JPSP.pdf
6. Allen, 'The Science of Gratitude', ibid.

4. Learning to spend mindfully

1. Glennon Doyle, *Untamed: Stop Pleasing, Start Living* ibid.
2. Aka Barber, *Consumed* (Brazen, 2021).
3. Otegha Uwagba, *We Need to Talk about Money* (Fourth Estate, 2021).

5. Planning and preparing for the future

1. https://www.goodmoneyweek.com/sites/default/files/
   download/_gmw2020_consumer_guide_2.pdf
2. https://www.theguardian.com/society/2018/may/09/
   mental-health-crisis-generation-rent-millennials-own-
   home-wellbeing
3. Rhiannon Lucy Cosslet, '"I have sleepless nights": the
   looming mental health crisis facing generation rent',
   Guardian, 9 May 2018, https://www.employeebenefits.
   co.uk/uk-gender-pensions-gap-averages-38/
4. 'The underpensioned report 2020: Examining the
   pension savings gaps for the most financially at-risk
   groups in our society', https://www.fairpensionsforall.
   com/wp-content/uploads/2020/12/NP000_
   Underpension_report_Nov2020-1.pdf
5. 'How to find lost pensions with a NI number', *Telegraph*,
   10 June 2021, https://www.telegraph.co.uk/financial-
   services/pensions-advice-service/find-my-pension/

Further Reading

On money, culture and consumption

Aja Barber, *Consumed: The Need for Collective Change: Colonialism, Climate Change & Consumerism* (Octopus, 2021)

Alex Holder, *Open Up: Why talking About Money Will Change Your Life* (Serpent's Tail, 2019)

Otegha Uwagba, *We Need to Talk about Money* (Fourth Estate, 2021)

On money management and investing

Emilie Bellet, *You're Not Broke, You're Pre-Rich: How to Streamline Your Finances, Stay in Control of Your Bank Balance and Have More £££* (Octopus, 2019)

Selina Flavius, *Black Girl Finance: Let's Talk Money* (Quercus, 2021)

On work and worth

Anna Codrea-Rado, *You're the Business: How to Build a Successful Career When You Strike Out Alone* (Virgin Books, 2021)

Elizabeth Uviebinene, *The Reset: Ideas to Change How We Work and Live* (Hodder & Stoughton, 2021)

On boundaries

Nedra Glover Tawwab, *Set Boundaries, Find Peace: A Guide to Reclaiming Yourself* (Piatkus, 2020)

On self-worth

Anna Mathur, *Know Your Worth: How to Build Your Self-esteem, Grow in Confidence and Worry Less About What People Think* (Piatkus, 2021)

Glennon Doyle, *Untamed: Stop Pleasing, Start Living* (Vermillion, 2020)

Jo Love, *Therapy is Magic: An Essential Guide to the Ups, Downs and Life-Changing Experiences of Talking Therapy* (Bluebird, 2021)

On habits

James Clear, *Atomic Habits: An Easy & Proven Way to Build Good Habits & Break Bad Ones* (Random House Business, 2018)

On gratitude

Robert Emmons, *Thanks!: How Practicing Gratitude Can Make You Happier* (Mariner Books, 2008)

On self-care

Suzy Reading, *The Self-care Revolution: Smart Habits & Simple Practices to Allow You to Flourish* (Aster, 2017)

Suzy Reading, *Self-care for Tough Times: How to Heal in Times of Anxiety, Loss and Change* (Aster, 2021)

On happiness

Mo Gawdat, *Solve for Happy: Engineer Your Path to Joy* (Bluebird, 2019)

Owen O'Kane, *Ten to Zen: Ten Minutes a Day to a Calmer, Happier You* (Bluebird, 2018)

Acknowledgements

The person I must thank most for making this book possible is, without doubt, my editor Anna Steadman. There were times when writing felt impossible, when I lost confidence in both my ideas and my place as the author of this book, and you always knew just when to push and when to encourage, and when to allow me to draw my own conclusions about what was missing. I feel so lucky to have been able to work with you again. Similarly, I owe huge thanks to my agent, Julia Silk, for running through the various iterations and ideas for this book with me and helping me to figure out what it should be, and for never complaining when a quick catch-up turned into over an hour on the phone. To Daisy Buchanan, thank you for your notes of encouragement, and to Otegha Uwagba, thank you for the never-ending food for thought. To the many contributors – Jo Love, Aja Barber, Suzy Reading and Anna Codrea-Rado, thank you for your insights and wisdom, and to everyone who shared something personal about their relationship with money with me, I am eternally grateful for your openness and candour.

To everyone who propped me up during the pandemic – my mum, Fiona, Pete, Chloe, Stef, Lucy, Sam, Hayley, Kathryn and more – thank you for helping me to stay sane enough to write. To Dr Ezobi, thank you for throwing me a lifeline when everything went suddenly dark. To my boys, thank you for loving me and each other so fiercely, and for being so brilliantly yourselves. Thank you for giving me a reason to get up in the morning when it felt impossible. To Phil, thank you for being my anchor. Without you, I am entirely adrift.

Index

About the author

When Clare Seal reached what seemed like a breaking point in her relationship with money in spring 2019, she turned to Instagram to make herself accountable, posting anonymously about her journey out of debt as @myfrugalyear. She immediately struck a chord, with her posts offering advice and solidarity to a growing community of people in a similar situation. Now an established voice on the finance scene, Clare Seal writes a regular column for *Glamour* and also runs The Financial Wellbeing Forum (www.thefwforum.com), providing articles, online courses, workplace education and workshops to nurture a controlled and confident relationship with money.